53½

THINGS

THAT · CHANGED · THE · WORLD

AND · SOME · THAT · DIDN'T!

BY
DAVID WEST

WRITTEN BY
STEVE PARKER

THE MILLBROOK PRESS
BROOKFIELD, CONNECTICUT

Steve Parker
Edited by
Bibby Whittaker

© N.W. Books 1992
Designed and created by
N.W. Books
28 Percy St
London W1P 9FF

First published 1992
by Simon & Schuster Young Books
Hemel Hempstead

First published 1995 in United States
by The Millbrook Press
2 Old New Milford Road
Brookfield, Connecticut 06804

Text copyright © 1992 Steve Parker
Illustrations copyright © 1992 David West

Printed and bound in Belgium
by Proost International Book Production

Library of Congress Cataloging-in-
Publication Data
Parker, Steve.
53 1/2 things that changed the world and
some that didn't / by Steve Parker: designed
and illustrated by David West.
p. cm.
Includes index.
ISBN 1-56294-603-X
1. Inventions – History – Juvenile
literature.
[1. Inventions–History.] I. West, David, Ill.
II. Title: Fifty-three and a half things that
changed the world and some that didn't.
T15.P358 1995
609–dc20   94-36649
                                  CIP
                                  AC

For Alan, Martin, Jamie and Oliver

THE 53½ THINGS

BEFORE HISTORY BEGAN 6
WALKING ON TWO LEGS • TOOLS • FIRE •
CLOTHES • ART • MUSIC • WORSHIP •
TOWNS • FARMING • WINES AND BEERS •
HORSE-RIDING • WHEELS • BRONZE AND
IRON • ARMIES • BOATS • POTTERY • GLASS
• THE RULE OF THE LAW • SCHOOLS •
VOTES FOR THE PEOPLE

...AND THINGS THAT DIDN'T 58

INTRODUCTION

Long, long ago (in fact, around 4.7 billion years ago), an immense cloud of gas and dust whirled through space. Slowly the gas and dust came together into a huge ball that was the Earth. It was so hot that rocks melted and volcanoes threw masses of red-hot lava into the poisonous air.

Since its very beginning, the world has been changing. Life began some 3.5 billion years ago. The first true fish swam about 500 million years ago. Earliest dinosaurs roamed the land 230 million years ago. And about two million years ago, another new type of creature appeared. It was the first human, *Homo habilis* or "Handy Man."

Using his clever hands and his extra brain power, Handy Man decided that he wasn't going to be pushed around by the world. He was going to change the world instead.

We are still changing the world today. The changes are happening faster and faster. It has truly become our world, full of our buildings, gadgets and machines. Since the first rock tools of the Stone Age, about 2.7 million years ago, we have been inventing things to make life easier, healthier, more comfortable, and more fun.

This book tells you about the 53½ discoveries and inventions that changed the world. Many are so important that, if they had not happened, we could not live our lives as we do now. Remember them all!

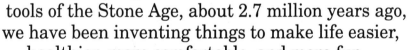

BEFORE HISTORY BEGAN

When written history began, about 5,000 years ago, people could record events and learn from the past. The time before that was prehistory. There were no written records. But there are remains – fossils, bits of stone and bone, ornaments and cave paintings, pottery and glass. From these leftovers we can piece together how people lived, and how they began to change the world.

Walking on two legs

In Tanzania, Africa, fossil-hunters have found footprints 3.6 million years old. They were made by two-legged creatures who walked like us. The prints are just like the ones you would make when you walk on damp sand at the beach. They were probably made by ape-humans called *Australopithecus*.

"Lucy," who lived in Africa just over 3 million years ago, was one of these creatures. Apes usually walk on four legs. Lucy's fossil skeleton shows that she stood upright and walked on two legs, like us. This left her front legs free to become arms, for carrying things and making things, such as tools.

— Modern woman

— Lucy

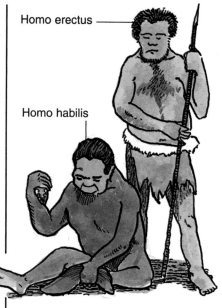

Homo erectus —

Homo habilis —

Tools

The first tools were hand-sized rocks and pebbles, chipped to give a sharp edge. They were made in Africa about 2 million years ago, probably by our distant ancestor *Homo habilis*, or "Handy Man." These tools were used to kill, cut up and skin animals for food. It was the beginning of the early Stone Age.

Gradually the tools got better, sharper, and more varied. By 400,000 years ago the next type of human, *Homo erectus*, had learned to make stone hand-axes, scrapers, cutters and chisels. These people could hunt a greater variety of animals, like deer and rhinoceros.

Fire

Some of the *Homo erectus* people lived in caves, in what is now China. In the winter, it was icy and snowy. But they weren't cold, because they used fire. Learning to control and use fire was an amazing step forward, after learning to walk.

Fossilized ashes, and burned wood and bones, show that those ancient humans had fires in their cave homes. They used the fires to keep warm, and to cook foods such as meats, berries and fruits. They may have used flaming torches to frighten away wild animals who tried to steal their meal!

6

Clothes

The earliest humans, such as *Homo habilis,* lived in Africa. They probably had hairy bodies, and the weather was warm, so they had little need for clothes.

Our own species, *Homo sapiens,* appeared about 40,000 years ago. They looked just like us, and they were spreading from Africa to colder places, such as Europe. They found that the fur coats of skinned animals, draped over their shoulders, kept them warm. Tie a length of vine around the waist, to stop the fur slipping off, and – hey presto, the first clothes! At last, they could go out hunting mammoths on a winter's day in the Ice Age!

About 30,000 years ago, in Europe and Western Asia, people were sewing furry skins with bone needles. They made fitted cloaks, tunics and leggings. By 6,000 years ago, in what's now Turkey, cloth was being woven.

Art

One of the earliest known pieces of art is a mammoth's tooth, worn by a person 100,000 years ago. It was probably a good-luck charm. Small statues and models of wild animals were being made by the early Europeans, the Cro-Magnons, about 30,000 years ago.

Soon after this came cave paintings. Some of the most beautiful are from about 15-20,000 years ago, in Altamira (Spain) and Lascaux (France). They showed that people were beginning to appreciate beauty and decoration, and that they had more spare time to play around with paints!

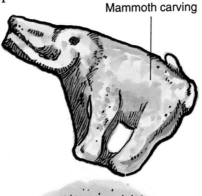

Mammoth carving

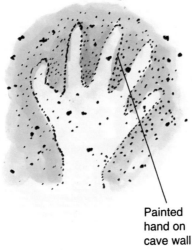

Painted hand on cave wall

Carved horse's head

Indian rattle drum

Reindeer toe bone whistle

Ancient Egyptian harp

Music

With the beginning of art also came the earliest music. In French caves, there are footprints made by dancers from more than 20,000 years ago, and bones carved to make whistles and drumsticks. One bone from a reindeer's toe, found in northern Europe, makes a beautiful flute sound when you blow over the hole in it. The people probably sang and chanted, too. By the time of Ancient Egypt, 6,000 years ago, musicians played flutes, harps and many other instruments.

Worship

Why bother with art and music? In the tough prehistoric world, weren't they a waste of time?

In the beginning, it's likely that art and music were mixed up with some form of worship and religion. This may have started as a form of remembrance, at the funeral of a loved one. Around 60,000 years ago, in present-day Iraq, people carefully buried their dead. They placed stone tools and animal horns by the body, and scattered flower petals on the grave. Another form of worship was praying for success in the hunt.

Why did people invent spirits, gods and prophets? Maybe they wanted to explain mysterious happenings. Gods could watch over people, and bring them rewards for living a good life. Also, the "chosen ones" who were in touch with the gods, such as priests and scribes, often had great power over the rest of the people! The first prophet of historical times was Zoraster of Persia, around 3,500 years ago.

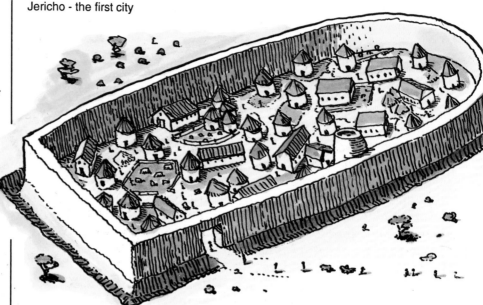

Jericho - the first city

Towns

Caves were cold, dark and drafty. Tents of animal skins and leafy branches could be blown away. About 10,000 years ago, people discovered that clay could be shaped and dried into bricks and stuck together. The first building site was invented, as people began to live in simple brick buildings.

Jericho, near the Dead Sea in the Middle East, is the earliest known city. It dates from about 10,000 years ago. By 9,000 years ago it had an outer wall over 16.5 feet high.

Why did people want to live together in a town? They could help each other, share the work, and develop their own skills. They could also defend themselves against dangerous animals and unfriendly people!

The first towns came before widespread farming. So it's likely that they grew up as trading centers. But soon, the countryside was about to change forever. Farming came on the scene.

Farming

The earliest people got their food by hunting wild beasts and searching for nuts and berries. It was dangerous, tiring and boring.

Around 9,000 years ago, people in the Middle East decided they wanted a change. They began to tame animals, and plant seeds. The tamed animals, such as goats and sheep, did not run away or fight. They gave milk, meat and wool instead. The seeds, like wheat and barley, grew into nourishing food crops. It was the start of farming, and of an easier, more settled life.

Wines and beers

Many fruits make alcohol as they rot naturally. In the search for interesting foods, some brave people tasted rotting fruit – and they soon felt happy and giggly. They had discovered alcohol.

Soon grapes were being specially grown to make wine. Besides tasting good, the wine helped to preserve other foods. The alcohol in the wine brought a good feeling, and freedom from worry and pain, although this wore off to leave a hangover headache!

The first wines were fermented in Mesopotamia, some 10,000 years ago. By about 6,000 years ago, brewers were producing beers in Mesopotamia.

Horse-riding

For thousands of years, people had hunted horses for food and skins. Then, more than 6,000 years ago, they started to harness the speed and strength of wild horses. Gradually the horses were tamed so that they could be ridden and pull heavy loads. This probably happened in the Ukraine region.

A few centuries later, Kurgan horsemen from the same area rode across Central Europe, speeding past their enemies. Horses were soon spreading to new regions, as carriers of soldiers and messengers, pullers of carts and chariots – and still as food!

Wheels

The first wheels were not on carts, but on potters' tables! In Mesopotamia, over 5,000 years ago, urns and bowls were turned with the help of a rotating solid disk. Then a bright Sumerian had the idea of fixing wheels to a cart. It was no longer such a drag to transport heavy things. Spoked wheels replaced solid wooden ones, and wheels have been rolling ever since.

Stone wheel   Wooden wheel

Spoked wheel   Iron wheel

Kurgan horseman

Bronze Age   Iron Age

Bronze and iron

Tools of stone, wood and bone tended to break or become blunt. In the search for better materials, people noticed that natural fires melted incredibly hard, shiny stuff out of certain rocks. These were metals.

The Ancient Egyptians found how to smelt and purify copper 5,500 years ago. Mixing it with tin, they started their Bronze Age around 3,000 years ago, although people in Bohemia had been using bronze 2,000 years before this. Bronze could be shaped, bent, cast and sharpened easily. The Stone Age was over.

Then some 3,500 years ago, the Hittites learned the more complicated process of purifying iron. Iron took over from bronze. It was harder and it lasted longer. Iron swords and blades were soon hacking off the heads of enemies!

Armies

People have probably always argued and fought each other. But gradually the rewards for a fight increased. The early towns and cities had valuable buildings, farm animals and crops, and works of art. Instead of making all these yourself, why not take someone else's? This was the beginning of organized warfare.

The Sumerians, 4,000 years ago, had wheeled war chariots. Among the most terrible of the early armies were the Assyrians, 3,000 years ago. They fought with swords, battle-axes, shields, bows and arrows. They tortured and cut up their opponents, and they won many of their battles simply by terrifying the enemy with stories of their cruelty!

Boats

The first sailors may have been driven by natural curiosity. They wanted to know – what's on the other side of the water? Boats were a way to explore and find new lands. About 50,000 years ago, the first Australians may have traveled there by boats, from Southeast Asia.

There are boats in rock paintings over 10,000 years old, in Spain, Scandinavia, and Western Asia. Around 6,000 years ago, boats with sails were being blown around Mesopotamia. They carried heavy things easily, and their wind power was free!

Through the ages, boats and ships have shaped where we live. Many major cities are ports on seas, lakes and rivers.

Early boat with sail

Early hide-covered boat

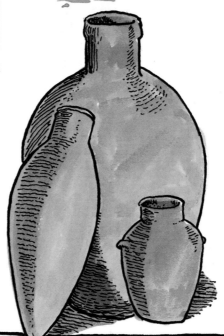

Pottery

Clay was "fired" with great heat to make it strong and hard, over 25,000 years ago in Central Europe. But the earliest purpose-made pots, jars, vats and bowls did not appear until about 10,000 years ago in Japan, and 7,000 years ago in the Near East.

Pottery became more widespread as a result of farms. After you produced the food, you needed to carry and store all your extra food for later! Clay vessels were ideal for this. Pots also allowed people to carry water from wells or rivers to their homes.

Glass

The Egyptians learned how to heat sand and other chemicals to make glass beads, almost 6,000 years ago. There was an early glassworks in Egypt 3,200 years ago. And around 2,000 years ago, Phoenicians learned how to "blow" molten (melted) glass to make hollow jars, vases and other shapes.

Glass was hard, smooth and easily cleaned. It became popular for ornaments and for storing foods and drinks – and you could see what was inside the jar!

(Glass windows, to keep out the wind and rain, have only become common in the past few hundred years.)

The rule of the law

Unwritten rules, handed down by word of mouth, have probably been around for as long as humans could talk. In wandering peoples, if a disagreement broke out, one group could simply move away from the other.

Towns and cities changed this. People wanted to stay in their homes, with their valuable possessions. Arguments and fights could start more easily. By 5,000 years ago, civilizations in Egypt, Mesopotamia, India and China had rules and laws. The idea of the laws was to keep people in order and make life peaceful. Punishment was harsh. You could lose your arm just for stealing bread!

Schools

Sometimes, you may think that school is boring. But imagine being taught nothing at all!

For thousands of years, people's lives were taken up with hunting, collecting plant food, and generally surviving. Children learned from their elders – or they perished.

As life became more complicated, new and more specialized jobs developed. The Ancient Egyptians and Sumerians had schools to teach their future politicians, priests and builders. The children learned about astronomy, writing, mathematics, architecture and government.

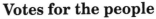

Votes for the people

Through the ages, many civilizations have been ruled by one person, such as a pharaoh, king, queen, emperor or priest. About 2,500 years ago, the Ancient Greeks began a system where the ordinary people could choose who governed them. This is called democracy, from the Greek words *demos*, meaning "the people," and *kratia*, which means "rule."

Today, many countries have democratic governments. The people vote for their leaders, who make decisions that affect us all. We, through them, can change the world!

THE TOILET

Yes, it's true. Once upon a time, there were no toilets. People left their – er, what shall we call them – body wastes behind the nearest bush. When there were fewer people, human droppings did not get in the way. They sure would today!

In the distant past, people did what animals do. They left their body wastes in the countryside, in a hole, or in a local river. The wastes were eaten by maggots, worms and dung beetles, and rotted away in the usual manner.

Gradually, there were more people, in towns and cities. The countryside got farther away. Body wastes began to pile up in smelly, rotting heaps, polluting the water and spreading disease. Something had to be done.

ROMAN LATRINE

Wooden seats

Shallow channel

Water-filled trough

The hole in the floor

In ancient times, people had special seats with holes in, and pots beneath to catch the wastes. The pots were emptied outside. This happened in ancient Sumeria, Egypt and India, thousands of years ago.

Over 2,000 years ago, the Romans had simple toilets. Wastes fell through a hole in the floor into a sewer, where running water carried them away.

Look out below!

However, most people did not bother with toilets. They dug a hole at the end of the garden or in a field, and used that. As it filled up, they covered it with soil and dug another one. At night, they used a chamber-pot kept under the bed.

In castles, special holes were made in a wall or tower next to the moat. The wastes fell, plop, into the water of the moat. This was called a garde-robe.

Garderobe

Moat

Flushing

In the flush toilet, or water closet (WC), water from a tank swishes the wastes into the sewer. John Harington, godson of Queen Elizabeth I, had the idea in 1589. But hardly any houses had a water supply to fill the tank, or a drain where it could be emptied.

Two hundred years later, piped water and drains were more common. Alexander Cumming, a London watchmaker, designed a flush toilet. In 1778, inventor Joseph Bramah made a better one, with a cast iron bowl and a flap that opened into the drains. Bramah's closet was the first big-selling toilet.

Seat

MODERN FLUSH
LAVATORY

Stopping the smell

Terrible smells wafted from the drains, up the toilet and into the house. By 1849, Stephen Green had designed the U-bend or water trap. This curved piece of pipe, between bowl and drain, was always partly filled by water from the last flush. The water stopped the smells.

About the same time, ceramic (porcelain) bowls became popular. Their very smooth, shiny surface was easier to clean than iron.

Down the pan

Next was Doulton's pedestal water closet, in 1888. The water was stored in a tank or cistern on the wall, high above the toilet bowl, or pan. Pull the chain and water rushed down the pipe, around the bowl, through the trap, and into the sewer.

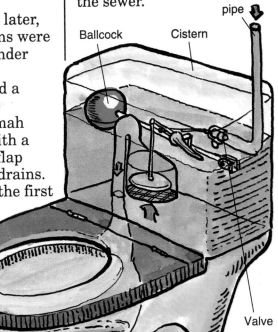

Water pipe

Ballcock   Cistern

Valve

Soil pipe

In about 1915, a new toilet design used the suction power of the siphon. It washed water strongly but quietly around the bowl. The water cistern could be placed much lower, just above the bowl. The all-singing, all-dancing, low-level flush toilet had arrived.

So that's where it came from

• In the last century, one of the most famous English "sanitary engineers" was Thomas Crapper. His company made toilets, washbasins and baths. Can you guess how his name lives on?

• The toilet became known as the privy, because it was a hidden and private place.

• The toilet is also known as the bathroom, powder room, water closet, rest room and john.

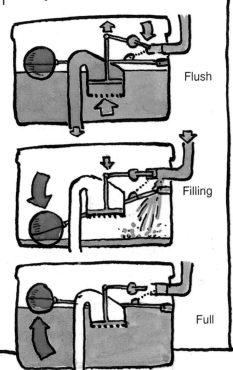

Flush

Filling

Full

THE BLAST FURNACE

How would you like to pull apart your food with your hands, and eat it with your fingers – at every meal? Knives and forks are just a couple of the thousands of things made from steel. Which is made from iron. And iron could only be made in large quantities when the blast furnace was invented.

In the beginning, people used stone, bone and wood. They wore out quickly. Then came the Iron Age, described on page 9. Iron was hard, and it could be melted, shaped, hammered and cast. But the problem was getting it out of iron ores, the natural rocks which contained it. For centuries, it was a slow process, and the iron itself was not very pure.

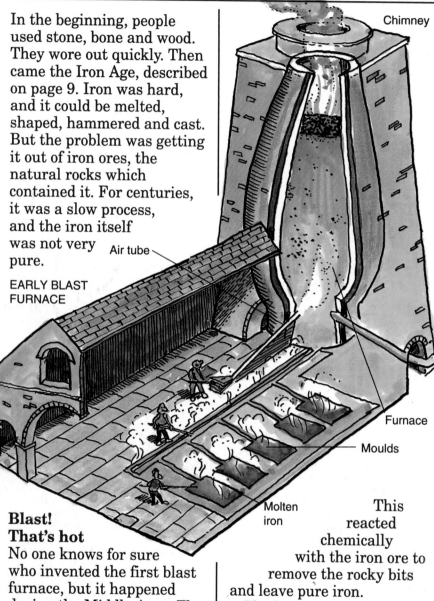

EARLY BLAST FURNACE

Chimney

Air tube

Furnace

Moulds

Molten iron

Blast! That's hot

No one knows for sure who invented the first blast furnace, but it happened during the Middle Ages. The idea was to heat charcoal, iron ore and limestone in a huge stone oven, at more than 1,832°F.

The charcoal burned with intense heat. As it burned it made carbon monoxide gas.

This reacted chemically with the iron ore to remove the rocky bits and leave pure iron.

The limestone absorbed the leftover bits to form slag, which was poured away.

The basic process was brought about by a blast of air blown up through the furnace to keep it glowing – the blast furnace.

More and more iron

By about 1840 iron-makers discovered that anthracite, a type of coal, burned hotter than charcoal. And if they pre-heated the blast of air, the furnace burned even better. The modern blast furnace was born. In the 1870s, coke replaced anthracite.

In those early days, a blast furnace made about 30 tons of iron each week. Today's blast furnace has a huge chimney-stack 98 feet high. It burns at 2,732°F, and makes more than 5,000 tons of iron every day, seven days a week. Iron is the commonest engineering metal. We couldn't do without it.

Iron facts

• Over nine-tenths of iron goes to make steel, for buildings, cars, trains, engines, machines, gear wheels, and of course knives and forks.

• The NatWest Tower in London is built on a steel framework weighing 4,000 tons.

• The world's tallest skyscraper, the Sears Building in Chicago, has over 80,000 tons of steel girder framework.

THE ROAD

Without roads, life would be very limited. It could take days to visit friends "down the road" – or rather, across the countryside – on bumpy, puddle-filled cart tracks. Without roads, our cars and motorbikes and trucks would have to stay in the garage!

About 5,000 years ago, people in the Middle East tried to improve their worn trackways by covering them with flat stones and gravel. But the first proper road-builders were the Romans, around 2,000 years ago. Their 50,000 miles of roads criss-crossed lands of the Roman Empire, from North Africa to Scotland, from Spain to the Middle East.

Roman roads had strong foundations, stone-paved surfaces, and good drains so that they did not flood. They cut straight lines across the countryside. Roman soldiers, chariots and supply carts could get quickly from place to place.

Modern roads

During the Dark Ages, most Roman roads crumbled away. The main routes became muddy horse-and-cart tracks. In the 1700s British engineers such as John McAdam and Thomas Telford began to build roads with strong stone foundations, a layer of hard-packed smaller stones over that, and a layer of hard-packed gravel on top.

With the coming of cars and trucks, from about 1900, the gravel topping was too loose. Modern roads have a variety of surfaces made from thick, black, gooey asphalt and tar, along with sand, sandstone, gravel, concrete and other tough materials.

MODERN ROAD

Gravel   Concrete   Tarmac

ROMAN ROAD

Stone slabs
Concrete
Stone lumps
Cement
Sand
Trench

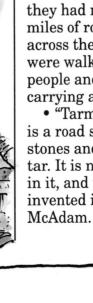

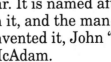

Well, I never knew that...

• Roads were not only for wheeled vehicles. In South America, the Inca people never discovered the wheel. Yet five hundred years ago they had more than 12,500 miles of roads, stretching across the continent. These were walked mainly by people and their load-carrying animals – llamas!

• "Tarmac"(tarmacadam) is a road surface of crushed stones and sand mixed with tar. It is named after the tar in it, and the man who invented it, John "Macadam" McAdam.

THE CLOCK

Tick-tock, tick-tock, tick ... RRRRRING. Darn the alarm clock. School at nine. Music club at four. Eat at six. My favorite TV show at seven. Why does bedtime always come too early? Time, and clocks, rule our lives.

In the old days, life was slower. There were no clocks. Tell friends you'd see them a day or two after new moon, perhaps before sundown.

Early time-keeping machines were very simple. Water dripped steadily through a hole. Marks on a candle slowly burned away. The shadow moved regularly around a sundial. It didn't matter. Hardly anyone kept accurate time.

Sundial

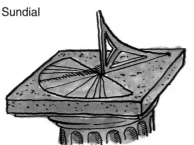

Escaping time
From about 1000AD, inventors made mechanical clocks. The fall of a weight on a chain was controlled by a bar with a point on each end, that rocked back and forth. Each rock let a gear wheel turn, or "escape," by one tooth — the verge escapement. It

was the start of tick-tock.
Famous Dutch scientist Christiaan Huygens designed clocks which used the regular swing of a pendulum, in 1656.

Around this time, exploring sailors wanted better clocks. Their navigation depended on taking readings at the right time, from the Sun, Moon and stars. Inventors came up with more accurate clocks called chronometers, or "time-measurers."

Christiaan Huygens

Good timing
By the 1700s, the wind-up clockwork clock was basically the same as we know it today. Modern clocks have electric motors, or vibrating quartz crystals. The best lose only 1 second in 50,000 years! We run our lives by the clock. How would you like it if your birthday party was three days late?

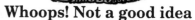

Whoops! Not a good idea
• For many years, wristwatches were worn only by women. Men liked bigger pocket-watches. But in World War One, soldiers realized that wristwatches were useful. Soon men started to wear them, too.

Watch pinned to sleeve

THE PIANO

Music decorates our world with beautiful sounds. It is a career for some, and pleasure for millions. Almost any music room or concert hall has a piano. Guitars may be popular today, but the piano has been the main instrument, for players and composers, for almost three centuries.

"Everything I do, I do it for you ..." Bryan Adams hit the top of the charts in 1991. The song starts with a piano. Almost all major pieces of classical music were written on the pianoforte. So are countless pop and rock tunes.

Hit, not plucked
The forerunner of the piano was the harpsichord, where the strings inside are plucked. In Italy in 1720, Bartolommeo Cristofori made a new version. The strings were hit by small cloth-covered wooden hammers.

He called it a harpsichord with *piano e forte*, which means "soft and loud." The player made loud sounds by pressing the keys hard, and quiet ones by pressing them softly – which the harpsichord could not do. The new instrument became known as the pianoforte, and eventually, the piano.

Cast-iron pianos
Early pianos were lightweight and not very loud. By the 1770s a new design, the English action, let the hammers hit the keys much harder, for more forceful playing.

In 1825, American

Alpheus Babcock designed a cast-iron frame, to take the tremendous force of the stretched metal strings. Pianos could be stronger and louder. They have hardly changed since then. But they have changed all types of music, from classical to rave.

EARLY SQUARE PIANO

Strings

Wooden case

Sounding board

Hammer

Five octave keyboard

GRAND PIANO

How the piano works
Press a piano key, and lots of levers move inside. The jack releases the hammer, which hits the string, bounces back, and is caught by the check and repetition lever. Keep the key down, the damper stays away from the string, and the note carries on.

Damper   String

Hammer

Jack   Key

Lever

Check

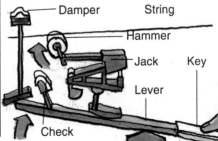

17

THE PLOW

How about a snack? Peanut butter sandwich, maybe?
Go out and find some wild wheat, grind its seeds
into flour, make your own bread. And find some
wild peanuts while you're out. Without plows and
planting, every mealtime would be like this.

About 9,000 years ago in the Middle East, the first farmers probably had bad backs. They discovered that if they broke up the ground first, and got rid of weeds, the seeds they planted would grow better. They used deer antlers or sharp sticks to hoe the ground. Back-breaking work!

By 6,000 years ago, the Egyptians carved a strong piece of sharpened wood, and pushed or pulled it through the soil. The power came from people or oxen. It was a simple plow, to break up the soil before planting crops.

The Greeks and Romans added a metal tip to the main plow blade, the plowshare, so it did not wear away so quickly.

Coulters and moldboards

The Middle Ages, around 1000-1200AD, saw several improvements. Wheels were added, to steady the plow for easier control. A metal cutting blade was added, too. This was the coulter, which sliced the earth in front of the main plowshare. Then came the curved moldboard, which turned the soil over, to give a fresh surface for planting.

Plows made completely of iron appeared around 1800. Oxen or horses still pulled them.

At the start of our century, along chugged the tractor. It became so powerful that it could pull lots of plow blades, in a gang-plow, through even the heaviest soil. Now a tractor-driver can plow more soil in a day than 50 Ancient Egyptians could plow in a week!

THE PLOW

Handle

Coulter

Moldboard

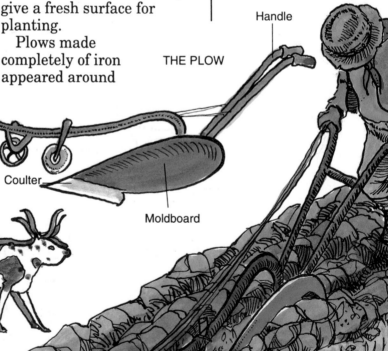

Get off my soccer field!
• In 12 hours, a modern tractor can pull a 21-blade plow through 150 acres of soil. That's about 75 soccer fields!

THE COMBINE HARVESTER

Imagine a harvest scene in the old days ... Golden autumn sunset over the fields ... Farm workers spend all day cutting and stacking bundles of wheat ... The next job is threshing, then baling the straw. Hang on, this sounds like hard work! Let's invent the combine harvester.

Harvests were hard work. You had to:

Reap When the crop ripened it was reaped, or cut, usually with sickles.

Thresh It was bashed with long-handled flails, to separate the grain (seeds) from chaff (unwanted bits) and straw (stems).

Load The grain was loaded into wagons, for the mill or grain store.

Bale The straw was tied into bundles, for animal bedding and food.

Combining jobs

Today, you have to: *Combine.* This huge multi-purpose machine combines the harvesting tasks. It does the jobs of up to 100 farm workers. It can harvest wheat, barley, rye or oats. With a few changes it can

deal with soy beans, rice and many other crops.

Tractors pulled the first combines over prairie fields, in the 1920s. Next they were made with their own engines. They were the latest in a long line of farm machines that took the hard work – but also the jobs and romance – out of harvest time.

Whoops! Not a good idea, at the time

• Andrew Meikle invented a mechanical thresher in the mid-1800s. Far from being thankful, farm workers rioted. They realized it could do their work quickly, and they relied on threshing as a winter job.

Reaping

Loading grain

Threshing machine

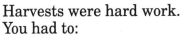

How the combine works
1 Reel pulls crop against cutting bar
2 Screw-shaped auger pulls crop towards threshing cylinder
3 Threshing cylinder separates grain, chaff and straw
4 Fan blows away chaff
5 Straw walker separates straw
6 Straw is thrown out the back
7 Grain is stored in a holding tank
8 Grain empties into a truck alongside

THE SAIL

"Ahoy, shipmates! There's a storm brewin'. Reef the mains'l (see note 1, below) and sheet the jib (2), or we won't splice the mainbrace (3) later!"
Before steamships, trains, trucks and planes, the sailing ships opened up new lands and trade routes around the globe. Today, they are used mainly for fun and racing.

The first sailing ships probably crossed the Mediterranean over 5,000 years ago. One rectangular sail hung from a crosswise pole called a spar, held on an upright pole, the mast. Wind power was free, and less tiring than paddles!

Phoenician merchant ship

Roman warship

The Ancient Egyptians were great sailors. So were the Phoenicians, with their galleys over 100 feet long. When the wind dropped, rows of oarsmen went into action. The Ancient Greeks and Romans used sailing ships to carry armies and supplies around their empires.

The golden age of sail
Through the Middle Ages and towards modern times, many different kinds of sailing ships were developed. Great wooden warships such as galleons had up to four masts and a dozen sails. They decided the fate of nations.

Fastest were the clippers, in the mid-1800s. They carried tea and spices from the Far East to Europe, and sailed to and from America and Australia. Some had over 20 sails. The clipper *Lightning* went 435 miles in one day. Some modern ships can't go that fast!

A lot of sail
• The sails of British battleship HMS *Sultan*, built in 1871, covered 2,630 square yards. That's the area of 12 tennis courts.

1 Reef the mains'l – Gather in part of the main sail, to reduce its area.

3 Splice the mainbrace – Get out the rum and the other drinks!

2 Sheet the jib – Pull the rope on the small triangular sail at the front.

THE SCREW

"Eureka! (I've found it!)" cried Archimedes of Ancient Greece, as he jumped from his bath and ran through the street. He had discovered Archimedes' principle, which has nothing to do with screws. But Archimedes supposedly invented the screw, too. It is used for irrigation, joining things, pushing along ships and airplanes, and opening wine bottles!

Over 2,000 years ago, people used screws to water their fields. Tar-covered wooden strips, in a corkscrew (helix) shape, were put in a tight-fitting wooden tube. A person turned the screw to push water up the tube, lifting it from a lake or river, up to the fields. Still in use today, this device is called the Archimedean screw.

Archimedean screw

Screws, nuts and bolts

In the 1600s, carpenters and craftsmen began to make their own screws, for attaching parts together. The woodscrew's narrow point gets wider, and its head has a slot for the screwdriver. In 1841, Joseph Whitworth designed standard sizes for screws; these were mass-produced.

Screw

Engineers also use the fixing devices known as bolts and nuts. Without screws, nuts and bolts, our world really would fall apart!

Ships and planes

The first ship powered by a screw, or screw-propeller, was made here in America in about 1804. It had sails, too, just in case. Screw-propellers were more effective than thrashing, energy-wasting paddles. 1843 saw the *Great Britain*, designed by Isambard Kingdom Brunel. It was the first big ship with a screw-propeller and an iron hull.

The Wright brothers used the same principle, but in air not water, for the first airplane (page 42). All early planes, and most small planes today, have propellers or "airscrews".

The *Great Britain*

Screwdriver

Bolt

Nut

Propeller

Paddle versus screw

• After much argument, the British Navy organized a tug-o'-war between a paddle-driven ship, the *Rattler,* and a screw-propeller ship, the *Alecto*. The screw won, and from that time, most ships were fitted with propellers.

THE TELESCOPE AND MICROSCOPE

Do you believe that the Moon is made of green cheese, and that germs don't exist? If you had a telescope and a microscope, you could see for yourself. Telescopes look at outer space, to reveal the mysteries of the Universe. Microscopes look into inner space, to show us what our own bodies are made of.

Many inventors and scientists messed about with curved pieces of glass, called lenses. From the 1200s, lenses of various strengths were used in eyeglasses. Two lenses, specially shaped and put near to each other, make distant things look bigger and nearer. This was probably discovered by Hans Lippershey in Holland, in 1608.

Early spectacles

Within a year, the famous Galileo heard about the new invention, and made his own versions. They magnified up to 30 times. He scanned the dark skies and discovered mountains on the Moon, spots on the Sun, and moons going round Jupiter. He was the first real telescope-user.

Galileo

Types of telescopes

Christiaan Huygens, who worked on pendulum clocks (page 16), also invented better telescopes. In about 1757 a British optician, John Dollond, sandwiched two lenses closely together. These compound lenses gave better, clearer images.

In 1668 the great Isaac Newton designed a telescope with a curved mirror in place of one lens. This was called a reflector. Today, the biggest optical telescopes are reflectors. They look deep into space, to tell us about our Moon and Sun, the planets and stars, and the beginning of the Universe.

REFRACTING LENS TELESCOPE

Isaac Newton

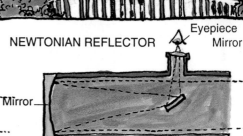

Telescope focused by moving extensions

Extensions

Observatory

GALILEO'S TELESCOPE

Eyepiece lens

REFRACTING LENS TELESCOPE

Convex lens

Mirror

NEWTONIAN REFLECTOR

Eyepiece Mirror

Eyepiece lens

Seeing the invisible

Around 1590, Dutch lens-maker Zacharias Janssen also put two lenses near to each other. He noticed that a tiny thing at one end looked much bigger from the other end – provided the lenses were the right distance apart.

Scientists showed an interest. They realized that a whole tiny world was waiting to be discovered. In 1655, Robert Hooke first used the word "cell" for a microscopic part of a living thing, in his book Micrographia, "Small Drawings." Hooke showed that tiny creatures such as ants had a heart, stomach and other body parts – just like bigger animals, but smaller!

LEEUWENHOEK'S MICROSCOPE

Lens

Object

Draper turned lens-maker

By the 1680s Anton van Leeuwenhoek, in Holland, made fascinating discoveries through the microscope. His homemade microscopes could magnify over 250 times. Through them he saw new wonders such as red blood cells, tiny one-celled creatures like amoebas, the eggs of fleas, insect eyes, and stacks of cells in the thinnest leaf.

Anton van Leeuwenhoek

After Leeuwenhoek, many people looked through microscopes. The science of microbiology began. Soon people were looking at germs, and working out how they invaded the body and caused diseases.

Microscopes became more powerful, with strong lights and changeable lenses that could magnify over one thousand times. Today, medicine and biology would be lost without microscopes.

MODERN MICROSCOPE

Eyepiece

Lens

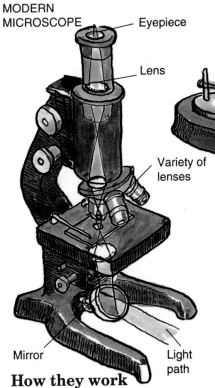

Variety of lenses

Mirror

Light path

How they work

In a microscope, light waves from the tiny and nearby object are bent inwards by the convex (bulging) lens. They are bent again at the second lens, the eyepiece, so that you see a clear and enlarged view.

In a telescope, much the same happens. But the light waves come from far, far away, so they are parallel when they reach the telescope.

EARLY MICROSCOPE

Eyepiece

Metal body

Focusing screw

Object

Wow! Big, small, and far-out

• The telescope with the biggest one-piece lens is at the Yerkes Observatory, in the USA. The lens is 40 inches across.

• Electron microscopes use electron beams instead of light rays. They magnify over one million times.

• Radio telescopes detect not light rays, but radio waves from stars, quasars and pulsars. They can "see" billions of miles, to the far side of the Universe.

Radio telescopes

THE PRINTING PRESS

If printing had never been invented, then

...Exactly!!

The year: 1455. The place: Mainz, Germany. The person: Johann Gutenberg. The result: about 300 copies of what we now call the Gutenberg Bible, the first full-length book made on a proper mechanical printing press. It had 1,284 pages, two columns on each page, 42 lines in each column. Fewer than 50 copies survive.

Johann Gutenberg

We see printed words and drawings and photographs not only in books. They are in newspapers and magazines, on containers and labels, on billboards, even on T-shirts, almost everywhere! Printing is central to the way we learn. Imagine life without school textbooks! (Then again, don't.)

One copy at a time

There was printing five centuries before Gutenberg. In China, shapes of pictures and writing were cut onto wood or stone blocks. Printers spread ink on the block, pressed paper on it, and the ink on the raised bits stuck to the paper. They could make many prints from one block.

Early printing block

But each new work needed a new block. So a system was developed with small metal blocks, which could be moved and arranged in different orders. However, the complicated Chinese writing system, with thousands of symbols, meant slow progress.

Early Chinese

There were also hand-made books before Gutenberg. Monks, especially, spent years writing and decorating the letters by hand, with pens, one beautiful book at a time.

Moveable type

Gutenberg and his helpers produced hundreds of small metal blocks, each with a raised part of one letter or symbol, in reverse. The letters could be chosen and arranged in a frame, to print copies of a page from the book. Then a new set of letters was put into the frame for the next page. And so on, one page at a time.

Metal type blocks

GUTENBERG'S PRESS

Inking the type

Gutenberg Ink Inc

Another Gutenberg advance was new ink that stuck to the metal type, rather than to the usual carved woodblocks. And another was a powerful pressing machine that squeezed the paper against the inked type. It was adapted from a winepress, for squashing grapes!

Because the raised, inked letters were pressed onto paper, the method was called letterpress.

The letters and symbols were called type, and setting them up correctly was typesetting. For a long time they were placed by hand. In 1884 the Linotype machine made a line of type from molten metal that quickly went solid.

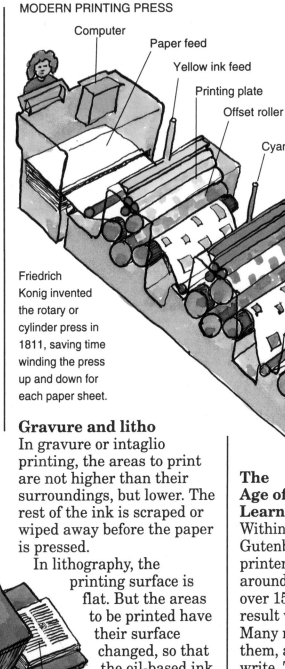

MODERN PRINTING PRESS

Computer

Paper feed

Yellow ink feed

Printing plate

Offset roller

Cyan ink feed

Magenta ink feed

Black ink feed

Color pictures are printed from tiny dots of four ink colors: yellow, cyan (greeny-blue), magenta (reddy-purple) and black. Look at this one under a magnifying lens.

Friedrich Konig invented the rotary or cylinder press in 1811, saving time winding the press up and down for each paper sheet.

The press

Printed page

Typesetting

Finished copies

Gravure and litho

In gravure or intaglio printing, the areas to print are not higher than their surroundings, but lower. The rest of the ink is scraped or wiped away before the paper is pressed.

In lithography, the printing surface is flat. But the areas to be printed have their surface changed, so that the oil-based ink sticks only to them, and not to the untreated areas around. "Litho" was invented about 1796 by Aloys Senefelder. It is now the most popular kind of printing – this book was printed using litho.

The Age of Learning

Within 50 years of Gutenberg, there were printers in 200 towns around Europe, producing over 15,000 works. The main result was cheaper books. Many more people could buy them, and learn to read and write. Then they bought more books, read them, and learned even more. Schools and education changed forever.

Well I never!

• A printing system at the Lawrence Radiation Laboratory, California, can print the entire Bible in 65 seconds. That's 773,700 words!

MEDICINE

If you had a headache, would you let someone drill a hole in your skull to release the "evil spirits"? Medicine started like that! Most people nowadays expect doctors to cure them of life's aches and pains, and to heal serious diseases. Good medical care is sometimes not appreciated. It is just taken for granted.

Medicine began in the mists of prehistory. Some people found that they could cure an illness with a potion of plant juices, or a smear of animal fluids. They were the first doctors.

Some skulls over 10,000 years old have holes bored in them. The bone had grown back after being drilled, so these people must have survived after their "operation", trepanning.

A few early treatments worked, but many did not. Some were very harmful. Even so, if a medicine worked, people had respect and wonder for the doctor. As a result, doctors became powerful, and some were made into gods.

Trepanned skull

The father of medicine

One of the first proficient doctors was Hippocrates of Ancient Greece. He tried to rid medicine of magic and superstitions, and make it more scientific. He taught that a doctor's main aim was to help the patient, by finding the cause of an illness, and treating it. The results should be checked, so medicines could be improved. Hippocrates' main ideas are still followed today.

Hippocrates

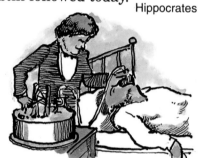

Deadening pain

Surgery has been around for thousands of years. The only way of deadening the pain of the knife and saw was to get the patient very drunk on alcohol or to use opium. In 1842, Dr. Crawford Long operated on a patient using ether as an anaesthetic, to deaden pain and other sensations. Today we could not imagine even a very small operation, without an anaesthetic.

Joseph Lister

Killing germs on the body

Until the 1860s, patients who had operations often suffered and died, because their wounds became infected with germs. British surgeon Joseph Lister began to use antiseptics (germ-killing substances) to clean his operating instruments and the patient's cuts. Within a few years, surgery became much safer.

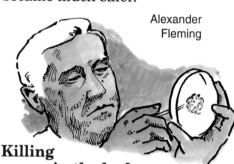

Alexander Fleming

Killing germs in the body

In 1928, British scientist Alexander Fleming discovered a substance which could kill bacteria (types of germs). It was made by a pinhead-sized mold called *Penicillium*, so he named it penicillin. This was the first antibiotic (bacteria-killing) drug. Many other antibiotics have been discovered, and they have saved millions of lives.

Seeing inside the body

X-rays were discovered by German professor Wilhelm Roentgen in 1895. People were amazed that they could pass through the body, except for bones. Soon X-rays were showing up broken bones and suspicious lumps and bumps.

Doctors have many modern methods of seeing into the body. CAT scans and NMR scans show the inside parts in amazing detail. Thin tubes called endoscopes can be pushed into the body, to examine and photograph the insides.

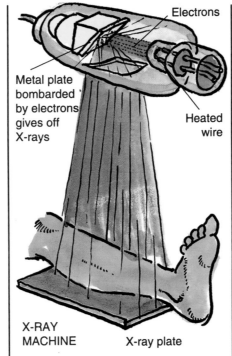

Electrons

Metal plate bombarded by electrons gives off X-rays

Heated wire

X-RAY MACHINE

X-ray plate

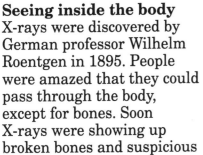

Broken bone

X-ray film

ENDOSCOPE

Eyepiece

Biopsy forceps control

Tube tip control

Water supply

Laser light source

Cat Scanner

Tube

Lens

Water jet

Light

Biopsy forceps

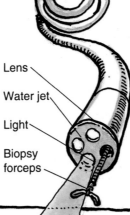

Whoops! Not a good idea

• Malaria is a serious illness spread by the bites of certain mosquitoes, which lay their eggs in water. Years ago, people thought malaria was spread by stale air (malaria means "bad air"). So they put sweet-smelling flowers in pots of water by the bedside. The mosquitoes laid their eggs in the water, hatched out and bit the sleeping people, and the illness spread even faster!

• "Ring-a-ring-a-roses, A pocket full of posies, A-tishoo, A-tishoo, All fall down." A nice nursery rhyme? In fact, it is about one of the worst diseases ever, the Great Plague. People kept roses and bunches of flowers, hoping the scent would keep the plague away. One of the first symptoms of the plague was sneezing. In a few days, most of them fell down dead.

THE ELECTRIC LIGHT

You are sitting quietly at home one evening, very interested in your school homework. Then pop, the light bulb goes out. Everything is dark. Before light bulbs, night was a twilight world of flickering camp fires, smoky candles, smelly oil lamps and hissing gas lights. Now we can turn night into day by flipping a light switch.

Inventor Thomas Edison came up with many bright ideas, like the phonograph (page 30). Brightest of all was the electric light bulb, in 1879.

Thomas Edison

There were electric lights at the time. These were mostly arc lamps, where a non-stop electric spark jumped across a small gap between the ends of two rods. Arc lamps were glaring, unreliable and costly. Yet people gasped with wonder, because they were so bright.

White-hot glow

Edison thought that a cheaper, better electric light would become popular and make him lots of money. He was right. The key was to find the best substance for the glowing filament. He tested hundreds, from platinum wire to fibers in bamboo stems! His first successful filament, of specially treated cotton, glowed for 45 hours.

LIGHT BULB

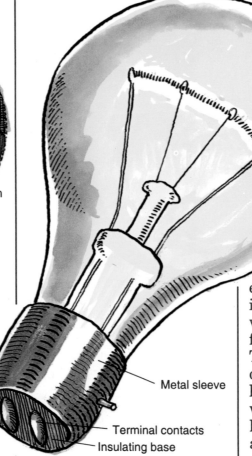

Glass bulb

Glass bulb is filled with an inert gas which stops the filament burning up as it would do in air

Filament

Metal sleeve

Terminal contacts

Insulating base

How the light bulb works

In a modern light bulb, the long, thin filament partly resists electricity flowing through it. As electricity forces its way through, it heats the filament to over 5,432°F. The filament (usually made of the metal tungsten) gets hotter than red-hot. It glows white-hot, and gives out light. A modern bulb lasts around 1,000 hours.

CLOSE-UP OF FILAMENT

English chemist Joseph Swan had invented a similar light bulb. At first he and Edison argued, but this wasted money, so they joined forces. In 1882, US factories made 100,000 light bulbs. By 1900, production reached over 35 million. Darkness was banished. Evenings – and school homework – have never been the same since.

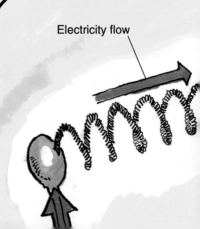

Electricity flow

THE ELECTRIC MOTOR

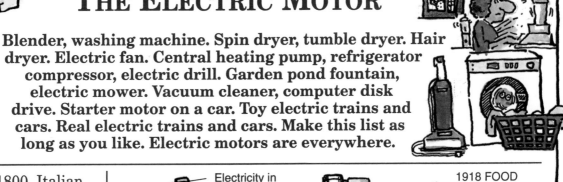

Blender, washing machine. Spin dryer, tumble dryer. Hair dryer. Electric fan. Central heating pump, refrigerator compressor, electric drill. Garden pond fountain, electric mower. Vacuum cleaner, computer disk drive. Starter motor on a car. Toy electric trains and cars. Real electric trains and cars. Make this list as long as you like. Electric motors are everywhere.

In 1800, Italian professor Alessandro Volta made the first battery. It gave a steady flow of electric current. But what for? No one had invented a machine to use electricity.

Volta's pile

In about 1820, English scientist Michael Faraday put a wire coil carrying an electric current near to a magnet. The magnet tried to move. He had the idea that electrical power could be converted into movement.

Michael Faraday

Faraday let a wire dangle near a magnet. When electricity flowed through the wire, it moved, and circled round and round the magnet. This was the principle of the electric motor.

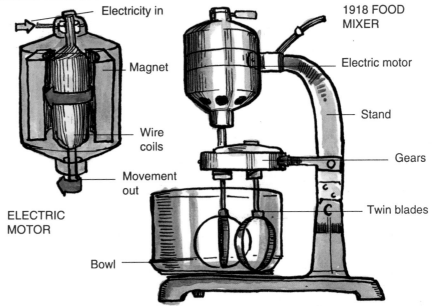

ELECTRIC MOTOR

- Electricity in
- Magnet
- Wire coils
- Movement out

1918 FOOD MIXER

- Electric motor
- Stand
- Gears
- Twin blades
- Bowl

Drills and lathes

In the 1830s, inventors built practical electric motors. Engineer Thomas Davenport made a motor to turn a drill, and another for a lathe. But the motors were weak and they soon used up the battery power.

From the 1880s, electricity wires were installed in some factories, offices and homes. Electricity was "on tap". It could be used to power electric motors, which soon became smaller, faster and cheaper. Motorized food mixers and sewing machines were common in the 1930s. Look around your house today, count the electric motors, and imagine doing all their jobs by hand!

Whoops! Success and failure

- During the Apollo Moon landings of the early 1970s, astronauts drove about on the Moon in a Lunar Rover. It was powered by electric motors and had a top speed of 11.2 mph.

- The Sinclair C5 was a small single-seater "car", powered by the type of electric motor used in washing machines. It came out in 1985, and was an instant flop.

THE PHONOGRAPH

"And this week's number one in the pop charts, with over a million sold, is *Fifty-Three-and-a-Half*, by Dave 'n' Steve!" The record charts, along with vinyl records, cassettes and compact discs, and the whole area of recorded music and speech, began with "Mary had a little lamb."

It's him again – Thomas Edison. In 1877, he had the idea of recording sound so that it could be played back afterwards.

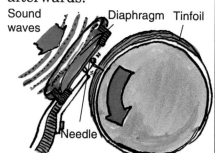

Sound waves   Diaphragm   Tinfoil   Needle

Edison designed a machine in which sound waves hit a thin, flat, metal sheet called a diaphragm. The waves made the diaphragm vibrate. The vibrations passed into a stylus or "needle." This pressed on a sheet of tinfoil, which was turning round on a cylinder. As the cylinder turned, the stylus pressed harder or softer for the different sounds, and made an up-and-down groove in the tinfoil. This was the recording.

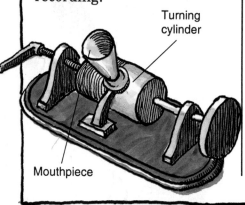

Turning cylinder

Mouthpiece

Groovy sounds

The recording in the tinfoil was changed back into sound waves by reversing the process. The cylinder turned, and the grooves made the stylus vibrate. These vibrations passed to the diaphragm, which shook the air around it, to make the original sounds.

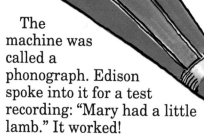

Horn amplifies sound

The machine was called a phonograph. Edison spoke into it for a test recording: "Mary had a little lamb." It worked!

Other inventors saw that the phonograph could be used for music and entertainment. In 1885, they used a cylinder covered with wax, instead of tinfoil. Lots of copies of one recording could be made, by pouring hot wax into a mold, which was shaped like the cylinder with its groove.

Cylinder to disc

In 1887, Emile Berliner came up with a flat disc, instead of a cylinder. The stylus was in a wavy groove and vibrated from side to side, rather than up and down as in Edison's version. Again, many discs could be made from one original recording.

Needle vibrates

Groove in disc

Berliner did not want his version to be confused with Edison's phonograph, so he called it the Gram-o-Phone. He gradually improved the sound quality. Soon people were buying the first recordings of songs. The "charts" had begun!

EDISON'S PHONOGRAPH

Drum

LPs to singles

Early record discs went round 78 times each minute, or 78 rpm (revolutions per minute). The discs were made of shellac. Vinyl records were introduced in 1946.

In 1948, the first successful long-playing records came out. They had much narrower grooves, went round at 33⅓ rpm, and lasted up to 30 minutes on each side.

Soon after, smaller vinyl discs came out. They usually had a single song on each side, they were seven inches across, and they went round at 45 rpm. They became known as "singles" or "45s."

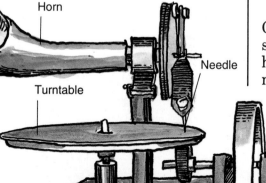

Horn

Needle

Turntable

Handle

Early 1950s tape recorder

Tape reel

Speaker

Tapes big and small

In the 1950s, enthusiasts recorded sounds as patterns of tiny magnetic patches, on a long tape. The big tape reels were awkward to handle, and they took a long time to wind up.

In the 1960s, the Philips company brought out much smaller magnetic tapes, in little plastic cases or "case-ettes." They were neat and easy to handle. You could buy them already recorded, or make your own recordings. The cassette had arrived.

In the 1980s, compact discs began to take over. They had patterns of microscopic bumps and pits, detected by a laser beam.

If Edison could see all the CDs, cassettes, LPs and hi-fi systems today, he would be most amazed!

Tape cassette

Pits

Laser beam

1992 Sony Walkman

Aaaah, nice little dog

• The world-famous sign of HMV Records is a dog listening to the sound from a gramophone. This was a real dog, that lived in about 1900. Its owner had made a gramophone recording, but then died. When the recording played, the dog came over and sadly listened to – His Master's Voice.

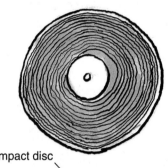

• How many grooves on a vinyl record? Two – a very long one on each side!

Compact disc

GUNS AND GUNPOWDER

Bang! Crack! BOOM! The sound of gunfire echoes through the deserted streets, as freedom fighters battle with government troops ... Another war is about to change people's lives. Muskets to machine guns and cannons, in hands or on tanks, battleships and fighter planes, are still spitting death and destruction.

Gunpowder was the first explosive, invented in China about nine hundred years ago. It spread to the Middle East and Europe by about the 1300s. Set alight by a spark or flame, gunpowder burns all at once, in a split second, with a cloud of smoke, an enormous blast and a huge BANG.

Wherever gunpowder went, people used its destructive powers for good and evil. One method was to put a barrel of gunpowder next to the thing you wanted to destroy, light a long fuse, and get away. BOOM.

Matches and flints
The first guns were simple cannons, tubes of wood bound with iron rings. Pour gunpowder into the open end, followed by a tight-fitting stone or metal ball. Set light to the gunpowder through the small touch-hole at the closed end, and BANG.

During the 1400s, the matchlock was developed. It had a long metal barrel. Pull the trigger and a glowing rope hit the touch-hole, to set off the gunpowder. By the early 1600s a spark from a flint set off the gunpowder, in the flintlock.

These guns had wooden handles, or stocks. The stock let the firer aim properly, hold the hot metal barrel, and cope with the recoil or "kick" of the explosion.

MATCHLOCK

Sword, just in case

Glowing rope

Stand

Bullet | Sight

Rifled barrel

AK47 KALASHNIKOV

Gases push piston which cocks gun and ejects spent cartridge

Muzzles and breeches
Early guns were loaded by dropping the gunpowder and ball into the muzzle, the open end. This was slow and awkward, especially while the enemy was shooting back! Also, when gunpowder got wet, it did not work.

So percussion ignition and breech-loading guns were invented. Pull the trigger, and a hammer hits the percussion cap in the end of the cartridge, setting off a tiny explosion. This fires the main powder in the cartridge, which blasts the ball or bullet along the barrel. Cartridges were loaded through an opening at the back end, or breech, of the barrel. This basic system is still used today.

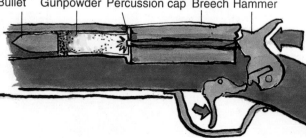

Bullet   Gunpowder   Percussion cap   Breech   Hammer

GUNS AND GUNPOWDER

Rifles and revolvers

"Rifling" is a spiral groove along the inside of a gun barrel. It makes the bullet spin, so that it goes straighter to its target. After breech-loading arrived, most guns could be rifled, and they soon were.

Guns dominated the Wild West. The legendary Winchester '73 repeater rifle was light enough to use on horseback. To speed up firing, small hand-guns were fitted with six-holed chambers that revolved around after each shot, to use the same barrel. They were revolvers or six-shooters. The most popular gun ever made was the Colt Single-Action Army Revolver, the "Peacemaker."

Rifling

Revolving chambers

Bullets

COLT REVOLVER

Penny for the Guy

• On November 4 1605, Guy Fawkes prepared to blow up King James I of England and his Parliament. Fawkes was in a Catholic group that wanted to overthrow the Protestant king and his followers. He put barrels of gunpowder in the cellars, below where the king would sit next day. But the gunpowder plot was discovered, and Fawkes was executed. In England they celebrate Guy Fawkes night on November 5 each year with gunpowder fireworks.

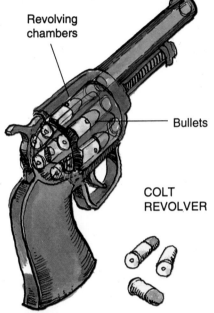

Firing pin

Chamber

Ammunition

Magazine

Trigger

Hand grip

Butt

Mikhail Timofeyenich Kalashnikov

The soldier's friend

Today, the gun is still the soldier's basic weapon. One of the best is the Kalashnikov AK47 automatic – fast-shooting, light, accurate, and devastating. Guns are also used for game shooting, as collector's pieces, and to keep the law.

Explosives such as guncotton, dynamite and TNT have replaced gunpowder. But guns still play a major part in world affairs, from crime-busting to winning the revolution.

• Until very recently Catholics and Protestants still shot each other in Northern Ireland.

THE TELEPHONE

"Can I order tickets for Friday by phone, please."
"Did you hear about the great party last week!"
"Emergency, which service do you require?"
"Hello, is that you, Mom?"
A world without telephones would be a difficult place. We could only talk to people and pass on urgent messages when they were in front of us. Even modern fax machines and computer modems rely on telephone lines.

For thousands of years, communication was face-to-face. Only a few simple methods, like smoke signals from a fire, or the beating of drums, could be used to send messages quickly across long distances.

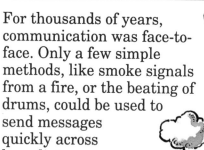

By the 1830s, battery power had arrived. People realized that if they had very long wires, they could send electric signals over great distances, using an on-off switch. The telegraph system was invented, and Samuel Morse came up with his dot-dash code.

The Morse key

Sound to electricity
Soon after the telegraph, inventors dreamed of making the electric signals copy the pattern of someone's voice.

Alexander Graham Bell was a doctor and speech teacher for deaf people. He knew about voices and sounds. In about 1876, he made a simple machine that changed sounds to electrical signals. The signals flashed along a wire, almost a million times faster than sounds went through the air. A similar machine at the other end of the wire changed the signals back into sounds.

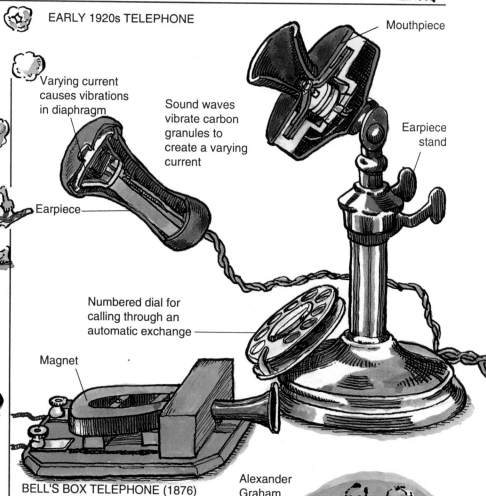

EARLY 1920s TELEPHONE

Varying current causes vibrations in diaphragm

Sound waves vibrate carbon granules to create a varying current

Mouthpiece

Earpiece stand

Earpiece

Numbered dial for calling through an automatic exchange

Magnet

BELL'S BOX TELEPHONE (1876)

Alexander Graham Bell

Coast-to-coast phones

In 1877, Bell showed that his machine could send signals almost 20 miles, from Boston to Salem, Massachusets. Within a few years, telephones were being installed in important buildings and in the homes of rich people.

At first, when you called someone, all the connections were made by hand. Operators worked switches and plugs in the local exchange. The first automatic switches arrived in 1892. By 1915, Americans could phone coast-to-coast. Today, many phone systems use satellite links.

All the same signals

There are probably almost one billion phones in the world. We use them for shopping, passing on messages, doing business, finding out information (such as the sports scores), and simply chatting.

When you talk into a telephone, it converts your voice to electrical signals. The phone lines can carry any similar type of small signals. So they can pass on signals from computers, teletypes, radios, televisions, fax machines and many other gadgets.

How the telephone works

A telephone has two main parts. These are called the mouthpiece and the earpiece.

In the mouthpiece, sounds make a flat piece of metal vibrate. This squashes and stretches tiny pieces of carbon in a container. Electricity goes through carbon pieces more easily when they are squashed, and less when they are stretched. So sounds are converted to very fast-changing electrical pulses or signals.

The signals go along the wire to the earpiece of the other telephone. They pass through a coil of wire, called an electromagnet. The magnetism produced pulls on a nearby sheet of metal. The strength of the magnetism varies with the fast-changing signals, so the metal moves back and forth very quickly. This makes the sound waves that you hear.

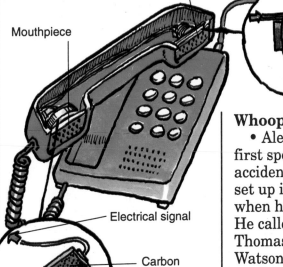

MODERN TELEPHONE

Earpiece

Mouthpiece

Thin metal sheet
Electrical signal
Electromagnet
Sound waves

Electrical signal

Carbon granules

Soundwaves

Whoops, a bit of trouble

• Alexander Graham Bell first spoke on the phone by accident. A test system was set up in his workroom, when he spilled some acid. He called to his assistant, Thomas Watson, "Mr Watson, come here, I want you!" In the next room, Watson heard the words over the test system. The first phone call was a plea for help!

• Many phones now have push buttons instead of a circular dial. But people still say, "Dial this number."

• Most phones have a bleeper or buzzer instead of a bell. Yet people still say, "Give me a ring."

RADIO

The air around us is full of waves. They carry messages and information on a vast range of matters, from weather forecasts to the latest news, from relaxing music to calls for emergency help. You cannot see the waves, or smell or feel them. But if you have a radio, you can hear what they have to say.

It began with numbers. In the 1860s, British scientist James Clerk Maxwell used mathematics to link light, heat, electricity and magnetism. He showed that invisible waves should be given off by an electric current that oscillated, or changed direction, many thousands of times each second.

Heinrich Hertz

In 1888, German scientist Heinrich Hertz built an electrical gadget to show this. Another gadget at the other end of the room detected the waves it gave off. It was the first radio transmission, over a distance of 9 feet!

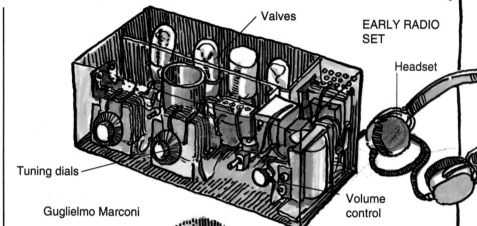

EARLY RADIO SET

Valves

Headset

Tuning dials

Volume control

Guglielmo Marconi

Across the Atlantic

The invisible waves are called radio waves. By the 1890s, Guglielmo Marconi was trying to vary them, like the electricity in a telephone varied, to carry messages. With no wires between sender and receiver, it would be "wireless."

Marconi sent radio messages across the Channel between England and France. In 1901 he sent them much farther, across the Atlantic, from Cornwall to Newfoundland. Radio spanned the world.

The first radio messages were Morse code dots and dashes. Then radio receivers were designed to change the waves into electrical signals and feed these into a loudspeaker, to make sounds. Home radio sets became common from the 1920s.

Radio waves are used not only by radio sets, but also by televisions, mobile phones, satellites, navigation beacons, radio-control devices, radar, and dozens of other devices.

Someone had to be first

• In London in 1910, Dr. Crippen killed his wife and escaped on a boat to America. Police sent a radio message to the boat in mid-ocean, and Crippen was captured. Radio had caught its first criminal!

• When Marconi died in 1937, the world's radio stations went silent for two minutes in his honor.

TELEVISION

Some people spend one-third of their lives asleep, one-third at work or school – and the other third watching television. Only fifty years ago, television was a new and wondrous invention. Try not to think of life without TV sets, computer screens and TV monitors of all kinds – it's too horrible!

After radio, scientists found ways to send pictures by radio waves, too.

John Logie Baird made a mechanical system in 1926. A wheel with a spiral pattern of holes whirled around. Each hole revealed a patch of light from the scene for a split-second. A light detector turned the patches into electrical signals, and a radio transmitter sent these as radio waves. The receiver was another whirling wheel, working in reverse.

John Logie Baird

TV milestones
Baird's system was used for a short while, but it had mechanical problems. The electronic TV system as we know it today was devised by Vladimir Zworykin, in the USA in the 1920s.

In 1936, a regular TV service (in black and white) started in London. A regular color TV service began in America in 1951, and came to Britain in 1967.

How the TV set works
Three electron guns at the back of the TV fire streams of electrons, tiny particles which are parts of atoms. When electrons hit the screen, it glows.

Strong electrical magnets bend the electron beams so that they trace a line across the top of the screen, then another line just below, and so on, to build up a picture over the whole screen. This happens 25 or 30 times each second. The result: very fast still pictures that, to our eyes, seem to move.

I'm a star!
• Baird tried his first mechanical TV in his attic. He rushed out and asked a passing boy to help. Back in the attic, Baird sent pictures of the face of the surprised boy – the first TV star.

Color electron guns

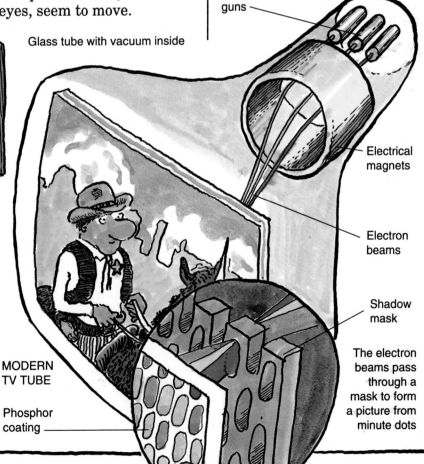

Glass tube with vacuum inside

Electrical magnets

Electron beams

Shadow mask

The electron beams pass through a mask to form a picture from minute dots

MODERN TV TUBE

Phosphor coating

THE STEAM ENGINE

Ah, the Golden Age of Steam. Locomotives puffing across the countryside, and steam-powered machines clanking away on farms and in factories. Watt happened to steam engines? They were noisy, dirty and inefficient, that's watt! So they aren't used much today. But for a time, steam power was the invention of the Industrial Revolution – which changed our world forever.

Hero, of Ancient Greece, made a simple engine using steam (page 44). But the modern Age of Steam began with Thomas Savery, an English military engineer, in about 1698.

Tin was a valuable metal. But the tin mines in Cornwall were often flooded by water seeping through the rocks. Savery's engine pumped out the water.

A fire heated water in a boiler, to give off steam. This passed into a large iron vessel, the condenser. Water sprayed over the outside, and the steam inside cooled and condensed into water. This left a vacuum, which sucked water up a pipe from the mine. More steam pushed the water away along another pipe.

Another Thomas

An English ironmonger, Thomas Newcomen, made the next advance in 1712. His engines pumped water from coal mines near Birmingham.

Newcomen's steam engine

The Newcomen version had a piston inside a cylinder. Steam was let into the bottom of the cylinder as the piston moved up. Then water sprayed onto the cylinder and condensed the steam, making a vacuum which sucked the piston down. The piston's up-and-down movements rocked a crossbeam that worked a water pump.

Guess Watt's next . . .

The father of steam

Yes, it's famous Scottish engineer, James Watt. He did not invent the steam engine. But by the 1780s he had made several great improvements.

One was a separate condenser, to change the steam back into water. This meant the main cylinder did not have to heat up and cool down all the time, which wasted energy. Another improvement was squirting steam into one side of the cylinder, to push the piston one way, then squirting it into the other side, to push the piston back. Yet another Watt advance was to change the up-and-down motion of a piston into the round-and-round motion of a wheel, using a connecting rod. Steam power had arrived!

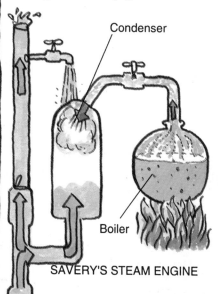
Condenser
Boiler
SAVERY'S STEAM ENGINE

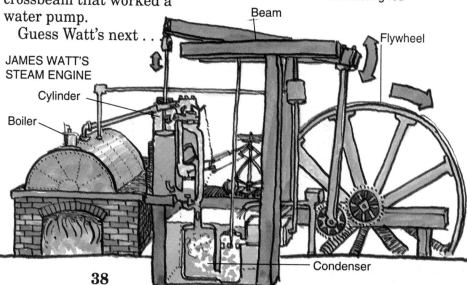
JAMES WATT'S STEAM ENGINE
Cylinder
Boiler
Beam
Connecting rod
Flywheel
Condenser

The coming of the railways

Richard Trevithick was a mine engineer in Cornwall, England. Many mines at the time had iron rails, for hauling wagons. Trevithick put railway wheels on a Watt-type steam engine and made the first locomotive, for mine work, in 1804.

Steam locomotives were soon chugging along the surface. The first steam passenger railway opened in 1825 between Stockton and Darlington, in northern England. Its locomotive Locomotion was designed by

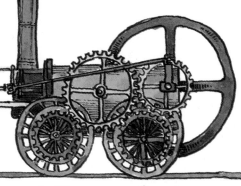

Trevithick's steam engine

George Stephenson. In 1829, Stephenson's better locomotive Rocket pulled railway wagons weighing 20 tons at 25 mph.

Many uses for steam

Within twenty years, almost every European country had a railway network. Steam engines were also powering cotton mills, iron foundries and a host of other machinery.

New forms of transport appeared: paddle-steamers and screw-driven steamships, steam-powered traction engines and tractors, and steam-propelled cars.

Steam engines turned the generators for Thomas Edison in 1882, at New York's first electricity power station .

Piston-power steam engines are rare today. But steam still generates most of our electricity, by whirling the blades of steam turbines.

Whoops! Not a good idea

• Nicolas Cugnot, a French soldier, built a three-wheeled steam-driven carriage in 1769. It was supposed to pull heavy cannons, but it went out of control and crashed. Cugnot's commanders decided to stick with horses.

• Another Frenchman, Clément Ader, made a steam-powered airplane called Eole in 1890. But the steam engine was too heavy for a plane, and it hardly got off the ground.

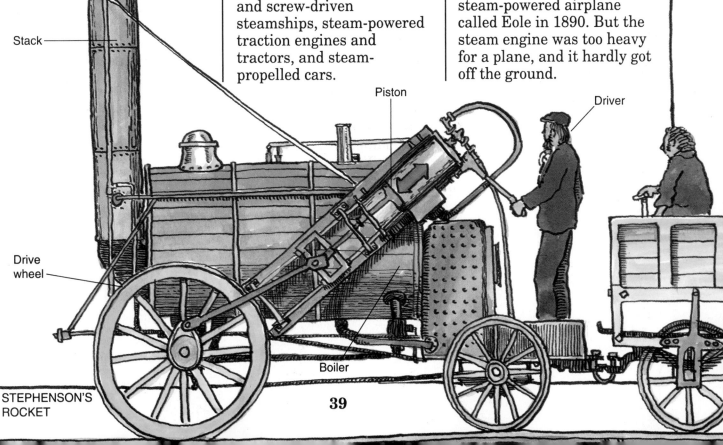

Stack

Drive wheel

Piston

Boiler

Driver

THE INTERNAL COMBUSTION ENGINE

Walk along the street. Niaooww – a motorcycle races past. Vrroom – a sports car chases it. Brrmm, a station wagon cruises by, followed by the ear-shattering Rrooaar of a juggernaut truck, and a taxi Dg-dg-dg. They are all powered by IC engines, an essential part of today's living.

What's an internal combustion or IC engine? You guessed: an engine that combusts or burns fuel inside it. The two main kinds are petrol (gasoline) and diesel. They vary from thumb-sized engines in model planes, to house-sized diesel engines in ships and trains.

IC engines can power motorcycles, cars, trucks, planes, locomotives, tractors, boats, home electricity generators, cement mixers, lawnmowers, hedgecutters and many more. Without their phutts, vrooms and brrmms, our world would be quieter and less polluted. It'd also be much slower, and harder work – no cars, and mowing the lawn by muscle power!

How the IC engine works

Like steam engines, IC engines have pistons and cylinders and cranks. These change back and forth oscillating motion into more useful round-and-round rotary motion. When the fuel burns in the engine, it creates tremendous pressure and pushes a piston along a cylinder.

The average gas engine is four-stroke, meaning the piston makes four strokes – two up, two down – for each complete cycle. It has four pistons and cylinders. Each fires at a different time, for overall smooth running.

SINGLE CYLINDER 4-STROKE ENGINE

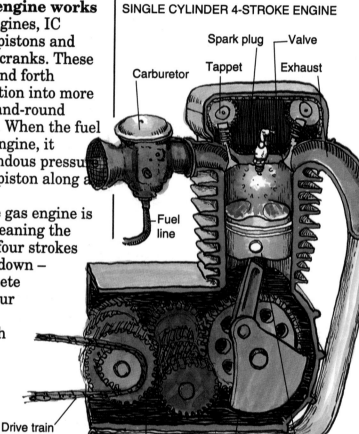

Spark plug — Valve
Carburetor — Tappet — Exhaust
Fuel line
Drive train
Gearbox — Flywheel — Piston

THE 4-STROKE GASOLINE ENGINE

Stroke 1
Fuel/air mixture drawn in

Stroke 2
Fuel/air mixture compressed

Stroke 3
Spark plug ignites fuel/air mixture

Stroke 4
Exhaust gases pushed out

Diesel engine

This has no spark plugs. It compresses the air more than a gasoline engine, which makes it so hot that when the fuel is sprayed in, it explodes. Diesel engines are usually more reliable and economical than gasoline engines, but bigger and heavier and noisier.

THE FOUR-STROKE DIESEL ENGINE

Fuel

Stroke 1
Air drawn in

Stroke 2
Air compressed

Stroke 3
Diesel injected and explodes

Stroke 4
Exhaust gases pushed out

Cars for everyone

The first mass-produced cars with IC engines were Model T Fords, made from 1908. They freed people from horses, trains, and legs, and let them drive when and where they wanted. They signaled a vast change in everyday life.

Cars were already around. The first modern-style car was the Mercedes, developed by the German engineer Gottlieb Daimler in 1900. He had already invented the first lightweight, high-speed, IC

Model T Ford

gasoline engine in 1883. Soon afterwards he fitted one to a bicycle, making the first motorcycle.

Also in the 1880s, another German engineer named Karl Benz built his Motorwagen. It was a 9 mph three-wheeler, powered by a gas-fueled IC engine – the start of modern motoring.

The first motorbike

It was a busy time. In 1892 yet another engineer in Germany, Rudolf Diesel, converted a steam engine and invented the engine named after him. It took him over five years to make a successful version.

Rudolf Diesel and his first diesel engine

Gas power and gunpowder power

Cars were not the earliest use for IC engines. The first practical IC engines ran on piped gas, and went nowhere. They were invented by German engineer Nikolaus Otto in 1876, and they replaced steam engines in some factories.

Even before this, in 1859, Etienne Lenoir of Paris made gas-fueled IC engines. They had spark plugs to explode the gas-air mixture, but they worked poorly and didn't sell well.

The first car

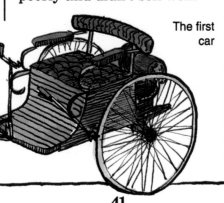

Seemed like a good idea at the time

• In the 1600s, Dutch scientist Christiaan Huygens thought about an IC engine using gunpowder-power! His idea came from the cannon, which is like a "one-stroke" IC engine. The ball is the piston, the barrel is the cylinder. The gunpowder explodes and pushes the piston along the cylinder. If the gunpowder could be quickly renewed and fired again ... just as well it couldn't!

THE AIRPLANE

If you had lots of money, where would you go for a three-week vacation? A tropical island, or a wildlife-packed rainforest? Without an airplane, it would take you three weeks just to get there! Airplanes made the world smaller. People can travel ten times faster than in a boat or train.

For centuries, flying was a dream. Brave men built bird-like wings and tried to flap from cliffs, only to crash to their doom. Scientific thinkers realized the human body was not designed for flight. It needed help.

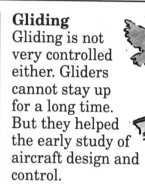

Lighter than air

The first person to get airborne was Frenchman Jean Pilâtre de Rozier. In 1783, he took off in a cloth-and-parchment balloon built by brothers Joseph and Jacques Montgolfier. The balloon was tied to a rope, and it rose because it had smoky hot air (from a fire) inside.

A few weeks later, de Rozier and the Marquis d'Arlandes floated freely over Paris in a bigger balloon. But this was not a true, controlled flight. Balloons simply drift with the wind.

Gliding

Gliding is not very controlled either. Gliders cannot stay up for a long time. But they helped the early study of aircraft design and control.

German engineer Otto Lilienthal greatly improved glider design. From 1891 he built over 20 types of gliders, and he made over 2,000 flights. But he crash-landed and died in 1896.

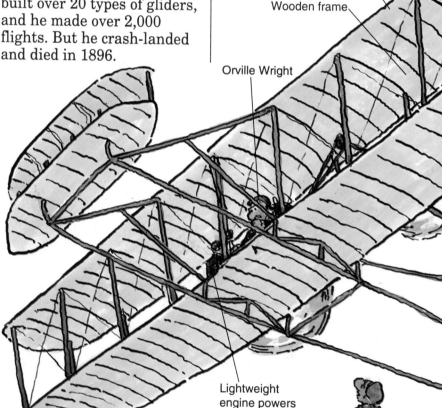

Otto Lilienthal

Cloth covering

Wooden frame

Orville Wright

Lightweight engine powers two pusher propellers

Wilbur Wright

WRIGHT FLYER 1

THE AIRPLANE

The first airplane

Lilienthal's death greatly affected brothers Wilbur and Orville Wright. For seven years, these bicycle engineers studied gliders and made model planes. They realized the steam engines and early gasoline engines of the time were too heavy for a plane. They designed their own lightweight version.

The Wrights built the first real airplane, the Flyer. Orville flew it on a windy beach near Kitty Hawk, North Carolina, on December 17, 1903. His first trip lasted just 12 seconds and covered 131 feet. But the Age of the Airplane had begun.

The Wrights' lightweight four-cylinder engine

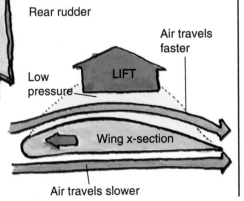

Rear rudder

Air travels faster

LIFT

Low pressure

Wing x-section

Air travels slower

Air travel

At first, planes were a curiosity. They put on shows for open-mouthed crowds. At the start of World War One in 1914, pilots checked enemy troop positions and shot them with pistols.

The first international passenger services began weekly in 1919, between Paris and Brussels. The first flight from London to Paris was by Air Travel and Transport Limited. It carried just one passenger!

Airplanes began to affect everyday life in the 1920s. Rich and important people could fly across a continent or ocean in a few hours. Air mail meant a letter reached the other side of the world in a few days, not weeks.

Today many people have a pilot's license and fly for fun. Planes carry cargoes and passengers to every part of the globe. A world without airplanes would be a much bigger place.

Private jet

How the wing works

An airplane wing is more curved on top than underneath. As it moves along, air has to rush faster over the top. This makes the air pressure lower on top, and higher below. It creates lift, and the wing gets "pushed" upwards.

Whoops! Better luck next time

• An early air casualty was the monk Eilmer, of Malmesbury Abbey, England. Legend says that in about 1000 AD he jumped from the abbey tower with small wings strapped to his arms. He broke both legs!

• Scientist, Samuel Langley test-flew his airplane, Aerodrome, a few weeks before the Wrights. It took off from a boat in the Potomac River – and crashed. After repairs, it crashed again. The newspapers enjoyed the failure. This is why, at first, people thought the Wright flight was a joke.

• Horatio Phillips' Multiplane had 20 thin wings, like a flying venetian blind! It made a few short flights in 1907. But it was very fragile and broke in half.

THE JET ENGINE

In the 1950s, jet airliners took to the skies. Air travel was becoming more common, and the speedier jets shrunk the world further. People could travel from the USA to Australia in less than two and a half days. Meanwhile, countries raced to get the fastest jet-powered fighters and bombers. Without jets, war wouldn't be the same!

A jet engine creates hot gases inside it, by burning its fuel in a sort of non-stop explosion. The gases blast out the back, and push the engine forwards. Since the 1950s, jets have taken over from propellers on most types of airplanes.

The first "jet"?

Around 1,900 years ago in Ancient Greece, Hero made a simple type of jet engine. His hollow metal ball could spin on swivels. He heated water in the ball. Steam rushed out of two angled nozzles, and made the ball turn.

In the last century, several people tried to invent jets. The idea was simple, but no metals could stand the enormous heat. In the late 1930s, World War II loomed. It gave aircraft research a great push. The fastest warplanes could help to win.

Hero's steam engine

The war of the jets

From 1930, English engineer Frank Whittle worked on jet engines. But the British government was not interested. Whittle had to work in an old shed, at the Royal Air Force base at Farnborough, Hampshire, England.

By 1937 Whittle test-fired his first jet engine, WU1, bolted on his laboratory bench!

Frank Whittle

Gloster Meteor

In Germany, Hans von Ohain and Ernst Heinkel worked on similar designs. On August 23rd, 1939, a Heinkel He178 became the first jet plane to fly.

It was war, and advances came quickly. The first jet fighter, the German He280, took off in April 1941. Britain's answer, the Gloster Meteor, was the first jet fighter in action.

The first jet-to-jet combat was between US Sabre jets and Soviet MiG-15 jets in the Korean War, 1950

Exhaust

Turbojet engine

USAF

The first German jets in action were Me262s, in September 1944. Pilots of the US 8th Air Force were amazed that these enemy planes had no propellers!

Me262

Peaceful uses

Jet planes came too late to have much effect on World War II. But July 1949 saw the world's first jet airliner, Britain's de Havilland Comet. The US Boeing 707 began carrying passengers in 1958. The famous Boeing 747 "Jumbo Jet", still the biggest jetliner, went into service in 1970.

TURBOJET

Turbine blades

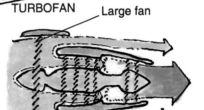

Compressor blades Combustion chamber Hot gases

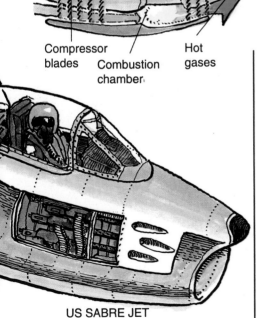

US SABRE JET

Jets to the rescue

The speed of a jet plane can whisk politicians across the world, take the sick and injured to the hospital, and carry emergency foods and medicines. Cargo jets bring exotic foods from faraway places, before they go rotten! Millions of vacationers fly in passenger jets to warm, sunny places. A type of jet engine, the jet turbine, provides the power for another essential machine, the helicopter. The jet engine shapes our modern life in many such ways.

Westland Sea King helicopter

de Havilland Comet

TURBOFAN   Large fan

How jet engines work

A turbojet has fan-shaped compressor blades, to squash the incoming air before it burns the fuel. As the hot gases roar from the back, they turn turbine blades which work the compressors.

A turbofan has an extra-big fan at the front, which blows air around the sides of the main engine. This design uses less fuel and is quieter than the turbojet. Most passenger jets have turbofans.

Jet record-breakers

• The fastest jetliner, Concorde, cruises at 1,450 mph. Because of the time change, if you fly from London to New York in Concorde, you arrive before you took off!

• The official air speed record is held by the US Lockheed SR71A "Blackbird" spy jet. In 1976 it flew at 2,193 mph.

• The world's fastest car is the jet-powered Thrust 2. In 1983 Englishman Richard Noble drove it across the Black Rock desert at 633 mph.

THE SPACE ROCKET

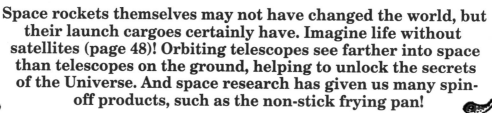

Space rockets themselves may not have changed the world, but their launch cargoes certainly have. Imagine life without satellites (page 48)! Orbiting telescopes see farther into space than telescopes on the ground, helping to unlock the secrets of the Universe. And space research has given us many spin-off products, such as the non-stick frying pan!

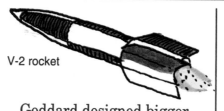

The Space Age began in 1957, when a Soviet A rocket launched the world's first satellite, Sputnik 1. But rocket research had been going on for many years before this.

The "father of space flight" was Konstantin Tsiolkovsky, a Russian schoolteacher. In 1903 he wrote a book showing how a rocket could work, but he did no experiments.

Sputnik 1

The first rocket

In 1926 Robert Goddard, an American engineer, launched the world's first real rocket at Auburn, Massachusetts. It used gas and liquid oxygen and went up only 40 feet, just higher than an average house. But it was a start!

Goddard and rocket

V-2 rocket

Goddard designed bigger, faster rockets that flew 1.2 miles high. Werner von Braun and his engineers in Germany did the same. Late in World War II, German V-2 rocket-missiles bombed targets over 120 miles away.

Man in space

SATURN V ROCKET

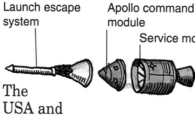

Launch escape system · Apollo command module · Service module · Lunar lander · Stage 3 rocket

The USA and USSR developed rockets for their long-range missiles. In the 1950s, these were powerful enough to fly 60 miles high, into space. To escape the Earth's gravity and float in space, a rocket must reach a speed of 25,000 mph.

The first spaceman was a Russian, Yuri Gagarin. In 1961 he took off in his Vostok spacecraft, on top of a Soviet A-1 rocket. First on the Moon were Neil Armstrong and Edwin Aldrin. In 1969 they took off

A1 VOSTOK ROCKET
Orbital capsule

Armstrong on the Moon

in their Apollo mooncraft, on top of a Saturn V rocket.

Most space rockets, like the modern European Ariane, burn up after launch and became useless. In 1981 NASA flew a new kind of re-useable craft, the Space Shuttle. It glides back to Earth from space, and can be used again.

Space spin-offs

Nowadays, rockets take off almost weekly. They carry satellites, space stations, experiments, deep-space probes and secret military equipment. Space research helps scientists to understand the human body, and to improve all kinds of delicate processes, such as making drugs and electronic circuits. The research has also come up with many new substances and "spin-offs." These range from better computers, to non-stick coatings on pans, silvery "space blankets" used by mountaineers and exhausted runners, "sticky spiders" that roll down a window, and plastic color-strip thermometers that tell you if you are sick!

SPACE SHUTTLE

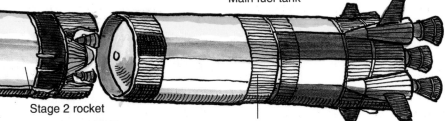

Orbiter

Main fuel tank

Solid fuel booster

Stage 2 rocket

Stage 1 rocket

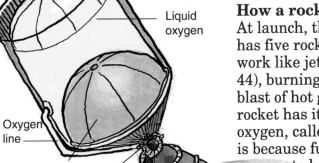

Liquid oxygen

Oxygen line

Liquid fuel

Engine

Nozzle

Whoops! Better luck next time

• The Apollo 13 Moon mission was in April 1970. Two days after take-off, an oxygen tank exploded and damaged the spacecraft. The astronauts reached the Moon, but could not land. They boosted straight back to Earth, returning safely four days later. Unlucky 13!

• In 1990 the US Navy test-fired a rocket-powered Trident missile, from a submarine under the ocean. The 32-ton missile left the sub, reached the surface – then went out of control, spun round crazily, and crashed into the sea. Back to the drawing board!

How a rocket works

At launch, the Space Shuttle has five rocket engines. They work like jet engines (page 44), burning fuel to create a blast of hot gases. A space rocket has its own supply of oxygen, called oxidizer. This is because fuel needs oxygen to burn, and there is no oxygen (nor much else) in space.

The Shuttle's two solid-fuel booster rockets fall off about 2 minutes after launch. The huge tank holds fuel for its three liquid-fuel rocket engines. The tank falls off 7 minutes later. In space, the Shuttle has enough fuel on board to fire its own engines and glide back to Earth.

THE SATELLITE

"And now, direct by satellite, we go live to the greatest music concert in history!" Our hi-tech world would end at once without space satellites. Global TV and radio, weather maps, long-distance telephone calls, ship and airplane navigation, spying on secret military projects, who's burning the tropical forests – satellites are vital to all these, and many more.

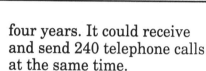

On 4 October 1957, the Soviet Union launched a rocket containing a shiny metal ball, 23 inches across, which held a small radio transmitter. It was the first satellite, Sputnik 1.

For three months it sent out a weak "bleep-bleep" to radio stations on the ground. Then it fell to Earth and burned up.

Satellites galore

A satellite is anything that orbits, or goes round, something else. The Earth is a satellite, orbiting the Sun. But when people talk of a "satellite," they usually mean something as big as a small truck, stuffed with electronics, bristling with radio dishes and solar panels and cameras, which a space rocket launches into orbit around the Earth.

Communications

Communications satellites, or comsats, receive radio signals from one part of the Earth, and beam them down to a wider area, or to another region. The signals may be TV or radio programs, telephone calls, computer information, or pathfinding signals from ships, submarines or airplanes.

One of the first successful satellites was Intelsat 1, also known as "Early Bird". It rocketed into space in 1965, and lasted

Early Bird

four years. It could receive and send 240 telephone calls at the same time.

A modern comsat can handle more than 30,000 telephone calls or over 25 TV channels. It weighs two tons, contains over 60,000 parts, and is powered by 17,000 sunlight-capturing solar cells.

OLYMPUS 1
Modern communications satellite

Rocket

Communications electronics

Gyroscopic stabilizers

Solar cells

Communications antenna

Altitude nozzle

Fuel

Metal foil

Research

Dozens of satellites are used for scientific research. Some look down on the Earth, taking special close-up or heat-pattern photographs, and pictures of clouds and weather. Others look deep into space. They get a much clearer view than they would from down on the surface. They detect light rays, radio waves, X-rays and many other kinds of rays and waves.

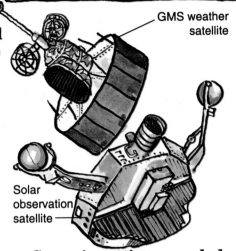

GMS weather satellite

Solar observation satellite

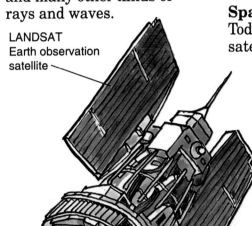

LANDSAT Earth observation satellite

Spy satellites

Some countries launch secret spy satellites to peer at others. They can identify and photograph a tank, fighter plane or missile launcher on the ground, from more than 60 miles up in space.

Military spy satellite

Space is getting crowded

Today, there are hundreds of satellites orbiting Earth. Space is vast, and there is only a tiny chance that one might crash into another. Even so, when a satellite is planned, the international space organization must be told. Then the satellite can orbit well away from others.

Hanging in the sky

Many comsats are launched into an orbit 21,600 miles high, where they speed through space at 6,600 miles per hour. Remember that, far below, the Earth spins once each day. In fact, these satellites orbit once each day, too. They seem to stay over the same spot on the surface, all the time.

This is called a geostationary orbit. It makes signalling to the satellite much easier. The ground stations do not have to track the satellite across the sky, because it just "hangs" in the same place, all day and night.

The ones that nearly got away

• In 1984, the crew of the Space Shuttle mended a satellite called Solar Max as it orbited high above the Earth.

• On another mission, they repaired Leasat 3.

• The Shuttle also brought back two satellites, Palapa B2 and Westar 6, to Earth for repairs. At millions of dollars each, a broken satellite is an expensive piece of space junk!

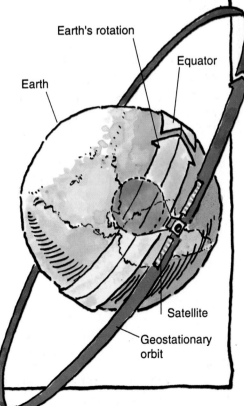

Earth's rotation

Equator

Earth

Satellite

Geostationary orbit

THE MAP

A map gives a bird's eye view of an area – from a few fields or streets, to the whole world. The golden age of map-making and exploration was about 1400-1800. If Christopher Columbus, Ferdinand Magellan and James Cook had not sailed the oceans and mapped the world, we might still think it was flat!

One of the first maps, carved on a piece of bone, shows a tiny area now called Mezhirich, Russia. It is 12,000 years old.

The Ancient Greeks and Romans were the first good map-makers. They sailed the Mediterranean and mapped its coastline. Their soldiers explored and conquered new lands. So they had good maps of Europe, North Africa and the Middle East – but not much else.

Mappa Mundi

Mappa Mundi

In the Middle Ages, a well-known map called the Mappa Mundi showed Jerusalem in the center of a flat Earth. Asia was at the top, Europe at the lower left, and Africa lower right.

In 1519-1522, Magellan's expedition sailed around the world and showed that the Earth was ball-shaped.

Since that time, hundreds of map-making expeditions have studied all parts of the land and the sea bed.

Plane carries surveying camera

Satellites can map large areas of land

Detailed surveying by theodolite

Ferdinand Magellan

Changing maps

Today, airplanes with survey cameras make ever more detailed maps. They show mountains and valleys, soil and rock types, croplands and cities. They are used by almost everyone, from highway planners to tourists.

Maps change. Wars alter national borders. Dams make new lakes. There are new roads, bridges and tunnels. Look at an old map, and see. Maps changed the world – and the world changes maps!

Old-time map-makers

• 3,500 years ago, Egyptian maps showed who owned the lowlands along the River Nile. This is because when the river flooded each year, it washed away boundary fences and marker posts.

• People once believed if you sailed off the edge of the flat Earth, you fell into the fire belching from the mouth of a giant dragon.

THE CAMERA

"Smile, please. Watch the birdie. Say cheese. Go back a bit more – oh, I didn't see that cliff!" Cameras take holiday pictures, photos for newspapers and books and magazines, home videos, and movies for the big screen.

The first camera was the camera obscura ("dark chamber"), a room or box with a small hole in one side. Light shone through the hole and was reflected down to make a light picture on a screen.

Camera obscura

Astronomers watched eclipses with them, and artists traced landscapes from them. During the 1600s, the hole was filled by a glass lens, to make the image clearer and brighter.

Capturing the image
From the 1800s, people tried to record the light image. They shone it onto a plate of chemicals. The light changed the chemicals, making a visible picture.

In 1826, Joseph Niepce produced the first permanent photograph, on chemical-coated pewter metal. In 1839, Louis Daguerre announced a better method using "wet" metal plates. However, each photograph was still a one-off.

In the same year, Henry Talbot's chemical-coated paper recorded the image as a negative, with light areas dark, and dark areas light. But it had an advantage. With more chemicals and paper, many positives – known as "prints" – could be made from one negative.

What a good idea!
George Eastman, head of Kodak, brought photography to ordinary people. In 1888, Kodak produced a camera loaded with film for 100 pictures. You took them and sent the whole camera back for processing and reloading. Next came the Kodak Brownie#1 in 1900.

It had separate, reloadable film and was even more popular. Suddenly, everyone could bore their friends with their vacation photos.

Brownie camera

Cameras
By the early 1900s, movie cameras were taking "moving pictures." The film industry began.

Modern video cameras do away with light-sensitive film. They record the light as tiny electrical signals, which are stored as magnetic patches on the videotape.

Joseph Niepce

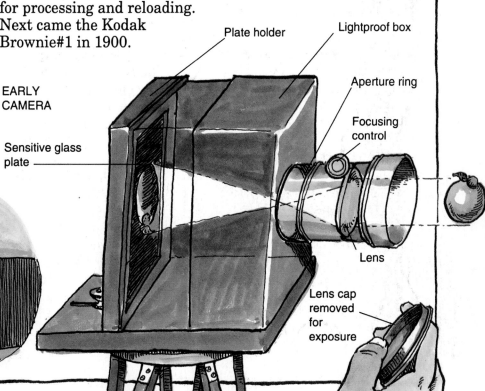

EARLY CAMERA

Plate holder

Lightproof box

Aperture ring

Focusing control

Sensitive glass plate

Lens

Lens cap removed for exposure

OIL

Drill into the ground, find "Black Gold",
Thick and sticky and not very cold,
Pump it out and get it sold,
By tanker and pipeline, to refinery,
Where the huge petroleum industry,
Oils the wheels of machinery.
Making plastics, asphalts, tars and wax,
Fuels for cars and trucks and jets,
... and stacks of other stuff!

Oil is so important in the modern world that nations threaten each other with oil bans, and fight wars about oilfields.

Millions of people are employed in the oil business, or petroleum industry. They search for it, drill it out, and transport it to huge chemical refineries. Here its ingredients are separated and made into a multitude of raw materials.

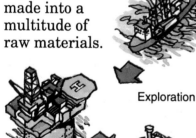

Exploration

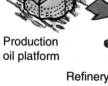

Production
oil platform

Refinery

A grinding halt

Without oil, the modern world would truly grind to a halt. Machines would have no lubricating oils, so they would seize up. Vehicles and planes would have no fuel. Millions of people who burn heating oil would get cold.

We'd have fewer plastics for electrical products, toys, plumbing and a host of other uses. There'd be no asphalt on roads, and no artificial fibers like nylon. There'd be far fewer farm and factory chemicals, glues, paints, detergents and soaps. No plastic bags, fewer carpets, medicines, artificial blood vessels ... Do you want more?

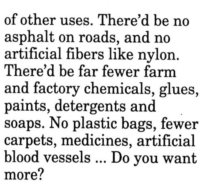

WITH OIL   WITHOUT OIL

Plastic
helmet

Wig

Synthetic
clothes

Mud flow

The first oil well

People used oils for thousands of years, for lamps, cooking, heating and lubrication. The oils often came from animals, such as sheep or great whales. Or they were scooped from natural oil and tar pits on the ground.

In 1859 at Titusville, in Pennsylvania, Colonel Edwin Drake and his crew drilled a hole into the ground. It took about two months. On August 27th the oil began to flow, marking the start of the petroleum industry.

OIL

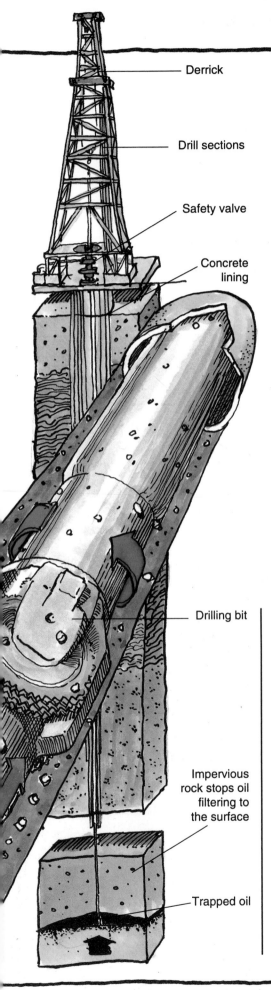

- Derrick
- Drill sections
- Safety valve
- Concrete lining
- Drilling bit
- Impervious rock stops oil filtering to the surface
- Trapped oil

Drilling

Oil is a liquid fossil. Millions of years ago it was tiny plants and animals, floating in the sea. They died, got buried, formed rocks, and slowly changed to oil and natural gas.

Drilling a hole to find oil is expensive. So scientists do many surveys and tests, such as making a mini-earthquake with explosives, to check if oil is there.

Then a huge tower called Derek – sorry, a derrick – is built for the drill. The derrick is on the land above the oil, or on a platform if the oil is under the sea bed. The drill has a diamond-studded bit and screw-together sections 30 feet long. The final hole may be 26,400 feet deep! When it reaches a pool of oil, the oil may ooze to the surface under its own pressure. Or it's forced up by pumping water or mud down the outer ring of the well hole.

Refining

The thick, dark stuff that comes out of the well is called crude oil or petroleum. It is taken by pipeline or oil tanker to the refinery. This is a giant chemical factory where oil is split into its components.

The crude flows into a tall tower called the fractionation column. This is hottest at the base, and cooler near the top. The various parts, or fractions, of the crude boil off as vapors. They cool and condense at their own level in the tower, and flow away along pipes for more purifying.

Wow, what a gusher!

- When oil spurts out of control from a well, it's called a wildcat. The biggest was in Qum, Iran, in 1956. It gushed 165 feet high, five times taller than an average house, and lasted 90 days.

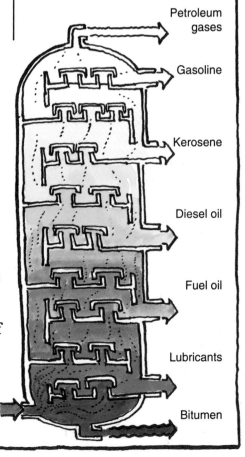

FRACTIONATION COLUMN

- Petroleum gases
- Gasoline
- Kerosene
- Diesel oil
- Fuel oil
- Lubricants
- Bitumen

ELECTRONICS AND THE MICROCHIP

Microchips aren't what you eat with a very small burger. They are hundreds and thousands of electronic components, on wafers of silicon smaller than your fingernail. And they're not only used in computers. They lurk in stereos, cars, washing machines, cameras, and dozens of other devices. Microchips are the latest thing to change the world.

It's the Electronic Age. Microchips and other tiny electronic devices affect almost everything we do, from switching TV channels to making a phone call. Our gadget-mad world is electronically controlled. And the speed of change is breathtaking.

Faster and cheaper
Fifty years ago, computers took up whole rooms. They needed air-conditioning, and enough electricity for a whole factory. A modern pocket calculator does more, faster, with a finger-sized battery.

Pocket calculator

Thirty years ago, an electronic circuit storing one piece of information (like a single number) cost more than $1.50. Today 5,000 of these circuits cost 75 cents.

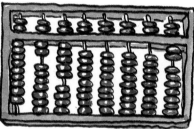

Abacus

Beads to valves
The abacus, invented around 300 AD, is still used in Eastern Asia. It's a memory aid for the user's mental sums. The column of beads on the right represents 1s, the next one is 10s, then 100s, and so on.

Colossus was an early computer which could be programed. It lived in Buckinghamshire, England in 1943, helping to break codes in World War II.

A famous early computer was Eniac, at the University of Pennsylvania, in 1946. It could do 300 sums each second, but connections had to be changed for each new type of calculation.

Valves to transistors
Valves were early electronic devices. They could switch, strengthen, reverse and alter tiny electrical signals. But they were as big as light bulbs, got hot, used lots of electricity, and tended to burn out.

Valve

Transistors arrived in the late 1940s. They did similar jobs to valves, but they were much smaller, more efficient, and faster. By the 1960s, battery-powered portable transistor radios were all the rage.

Transistor radio

Silicon crystal

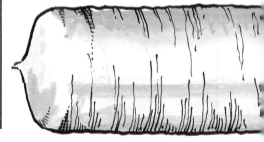

ELECTRONICS AND THE MICROCHIP

The coming of the chips

The first microchips appeared in the 1960s. They combined or integrated loads of components such as transistors, diodes, resistors, and capacitors into one circuit, on a chip of silicon – the "integrated circuit." It was a great advance.

Silicon is not a really good conductor of electricity, or a very bad one. It's a semiconductor. Wires, contacts and components can be made by etching patterns into a wafer of it, by processes using light or X-rays.

Computers

Today, microchips control the electrical workings of hundreds of devices. They save gas in cars by adjusting the engine, turn your video recorder on when you're out, and recognize magnetic codes in credit cards and bar codes in supermarkets. And they are vital to computers, which affect almost every part of modern life.

VDU

Keyboard

Mouse

Computer's central processing unit

Microchip

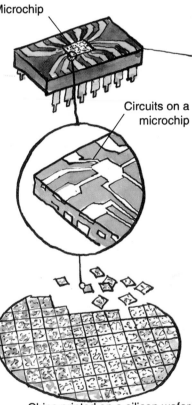

Circuits on a microchip

Chips printed on a silicon wafer

Silicon wafer

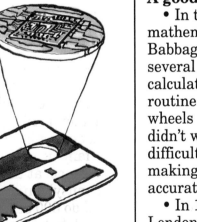

Microchip

SMARTCARD

Robots need chips to control them

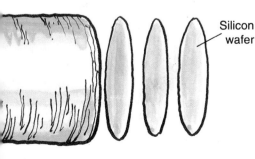

A good idea at the time

• In the 1820s, English mathematician Charles Babbage started designing several mechanical calculating machines to do routine sums, using gear wheels and levers. But these didn't work, due to difficulties at that time in making the metal parts accurately.

• In 1991, engineers at London's Science Museum built one of Babbage's machines. It worked!

THE ATOMIC BOMB

In a split second in 1945, the world changed forever. In the Pacific, World War II was dragging on. At 7:30 a.m. on August 6, the Allies dropped the first atomic bomb, over the Japanese city of Hiroshima. Killing and destruction were immense. In a few days, war ended. The shadow of atomic and nuclear weapons has been with us ever since.

"Little Boy" was a metal-cased bomb about 6 feet long. Exploding over Hiroshima, it killed some 75,000 people and flattened three-fifths of the city. Thousands more died later from injuries, burns and radiation sickness.

Little Boy

How the bomb worked

"Little Boy" had gigantic destructive power because it turned matter into energy. The matter was in the form of the radioactive substance uranium-235.

At the critical moment, two pieces of uranium-235 crashed together in the bomb. Some of the uranium atoms split, in a process called nuclear fission. The resulting atomic fragments weighed less than the original atoms, because parts of them were converted to energy – in the form of light, heat and radioactivity. The fission

Energy

NUCLEAR FISSION

also made more fast-moving atomic fragments, which collided with other uranium atoms, splitting them too, and so on, in a split-second chain reaction.

Nuclear weapons today

After the war, enough atomic bombs were made to blast the whole world to pieces many times.

Then came hydrogen bombs, which were even more powerful. Their energy was released when atomic bits of hydrogen joined together, in atomic fusion. Different types of hydrogen bombs form the bulk of today's nuclear weapons.

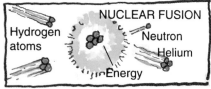

NUCLEAR FUSION
Hydrogen atoms
Neutron
Helium
Energy

Power to destroy

• One of the most powerful chemical high-explosives is TNT.

• An atomic bomb or A-bomb is a million times more powerful than a TNT bomb of the same size.

• A hydrogen bomb or H-bomb is a thousand times more powerful than an A-bomb of the same size.

FUSION POWER – *HALF AN INVENTION?*

A safe, cheap, reliable source of energy, that won't pollute the world or run out. Sounds like a dream? It has been. But in the 1990s, scientists are trying to make the dream real. Fusion power could not only change the world, but save it, too.

The hydrogen bombs described opposite work by nuclear fusion. But their energy is released all at once, in a massive BANG. Could the process be controlled in a fusion reactor? Experiments in the past few years show – hopefully, yes.

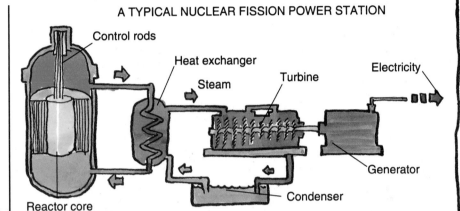

A TYPICAL NUCLEAR FISSION POWER STATION

Control rods

Heat exchanger

Steam

Turbine

Electricity

Reactor core

Generator

Condenser

Plasma-filled donut

A fusion reactor will be shaped like a donut, and called a torus. Inside, two forms of hydrogen called deuterium and tritium must be heated to an incredible 1,800,000,000°F, as they whirl around. At this temperature they are not solid, liquid or gas. They are another form of matter, plasma.

Some of the atomic bits in the plasma of deuterium and tritium join together, or fuse. They produce atomic bits of another substance, helium, and also give out vast amounts of heat and other energy. The heat could power electricity generators, as in a normal power station.

Copying the Sun

Today's nuclear power stations use fission reactors which split atoms, like the atomic bomb (opposite). In theory, fusion power could be cleaner, less dangerous and less polluting. But it will take many years and experiments before fusion power changes the world.

Even so, we already rely on it! Bits of hydrogen atoms fuse to form helium, creating light and heat and other energy – in the Sun.

Cold fusion fails

• In the early 1990s there was a great argument about "cold fusion", where fusion power might be made at ordinary temperatures. A few scientists claimed they'd got it to work. Others repeated the experiments, but they didn't work. No one has proved "cold fusion" since.

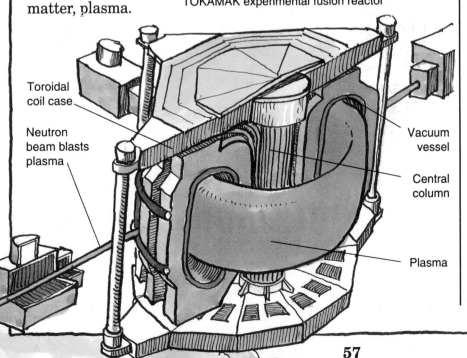

TOKAMAK experimental fusion reactor

Toroidal coil case

Neutron beam blasts plasma

Vacuum vessel

Central column

Plasma

... AND THINGS THAT DIDN'T

The bottom line is that humans can exist on just food, water and a bit of shelter. Things like cars, telephones, printing and music are not truly vital to life – even though, as we've seen, they have changed the world.

For every invention and advance that has altered the way we live, hundreds of others haven't. These inventions may be interesting or boring, serious or amusing, useful or downright useless. But they have not deeply affected daily life. Most of us could do without them. Could you?

The safety pin

This metal gadget was being used in Ancient Egypt over 4,500 years ago. It was "safe" because the sharp end of the pin slipped into a cover. Some designs looked like coiled serpents.

Early Egyptian   Modern

In 1849, Walter Hunt re-invented the safety pin. When a button or zip breaks, look for one. But how often do you find it? Oh well, back to the needle and thread.

The rattle

Toys are as old – or young – as babies and children. It's said that 2,400 years ago in Ancient Greece, the philosopher Archytas, a friend of Plato, invented the baby's rattle. He gave rattles to the families of slaves. He said that if children could make a noise, they would not break and wreck things.

Tame cats

You might argue that cats aren't tame. They only use us for food and warmth. Cats were loved and worshipped in Ancient Egypt. In the Middle Ages lots of families in Europe had cats, to kill the rats, which carried the fleas, which spread the Plague. Yet around the world, many other creatures live with people and keep down pests. They include mongooses, martens, dogs, jackals, falcons, even snakes and lions.

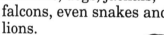

Man-carrying box kite 1905

Kites

Kites flew in China and Japan thousands of years ago. In war, they lifted observers high enough to spot the enemy. Scientists used them to take air and cloud samples. The highest kites were a row of eight, which rose to 32,087 feet over Germany in 1919. Today, kites still flap and zoom around the sky. All good fun, but not vital to modern civilization.

Napkins

In the olden days, people didn't bother to wipe their mouths or hands after eating a messy meal. As they became more aware of cleanliness they used tablecloths, and wiped their mouths on these. In the late 15th century, napkins appeared for cleaning knives, forks, mouths and fingers.

Chess

Chess, the champion board game, may have come from a game called chaturanga, played in India about 1,200 years ago. The chess pieces we know today appeared in Europe in the 15th century. The first proper chess book was published by French musician Francois Philidor in 1749. Millions of people play and enjoy chess. But life would go on without it.

National anthems

In modern times, the first country to adopt a song as its own tune was Switzerland, in about 1600. *The Star Spangled Banner* was written in 1814. France's *Marseillaise* of 1792 celebrated the French Revolution. There's still a good trade in national anthems, as countries fight and split and join and set up new states.

The umbrella

Ancient peoples used non-folding umbrellas against rain and sun. The modern version with folding metal spokes was developed in England in the 17th century, mainly as a parasol or sunshade. If you had an umbrella with silk panels, and a shaft of beautifully carved ivory, you were very rich.

The sandwich

In the mid-1700s, the Earl of Sandwich was so keen on gambling that he didn't want to stop for meals. Servants brought his meals of meat, placed between pieces of bread, so they were easy to carry. A snack was born. Lucky he wasn't the Earl of Wormtoad.

The rocking chair

American scientist and statesman Benjamin Franklin is credited with many ideas and inventions. A story says that in the 1750s, he noticed how a baby rocked in a cradle soon went to sleep. So he put cradle rockers on an ordinary chair, for grown-ups to rock themselves.

Aaaah, restful, but beware squashing your toes! Remember the old saying: "He's as nervous as a long-tailed cat in a roomful of rocking chairs."

Invisible ink

What's the use of ink you can't see? You have to make it visible by treating it in some way. Not by taking it to a movie, but by heating it or painting it with a special chemical.

An early invisible ink consisted of a mixture of milk and lemon juice, and was used in England, in the 1770s. Write and let it dry – nothing. But with gentle warmth, it turned brown. It was used by people to send secret messages.

Chewing gum

Thomas Adams, an American inventor, developed chewing gum in the 1870s. It was based on a natural rubbery substance called chicle, which oozes from the sapodilla tree of Central America. The Mayan people of Mexico chomped on chicle, a thousand years ago. Its chew-ability was rediscovered in the search for better rubbery substances for industry. Can you think of a flavor you can't buy?

Cornflakes

In the 1890s, the Kelloggs lived in Battle Creek, Michigan, USA. They were a large family – about 15 children. Will Kellogg, with his brother John, invented a method of toasting flakes of corn, to make a healthy yet cheap snack. In 1906 Will masterminded the Battle Creek Toasted Corn Flakes Competition. His company, Kelloggs, the makers of breakfast cereals, is still going strong.

Horse-racing on stage

In 1890 the Union Square Theatre in New York, USA, staged real horse races. Jockeys rode their mounts on a huge conveyor-like treadmill built into the stage. A man controlled the electric motors which moved the treadmill and the scenery behind.

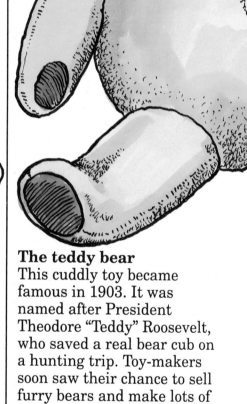

The teddy bear

This cuddly toy became famous in 1903. It was named after President Theodore "Teddy" Roosevelt, who saved a real bear cub on a hunting trip. Toy-makers soon saw their chance to sell furry bears and make lots of money.

Electric-arc iron

Smoothing irons were warmed over a fire or had a lump of hot metal inside. When electricity was first available in homes, around 1900, early electric irons had a carbon arc inside. Electricity jumped as a huge spark across the gap between two rods of carbon. It made an intense light, crackling noise, and heat. Luckily, it was soon followed by the heater-element iron we (well, some of us) use today.

ELECTRIC-ARC IRON

Carbon rods

Spruce Goose

This vast airplane was built in the 1940s by movie multi-millionaire Howard Hughes. It was a flying boat made of wood, with eight propellers and a wingspan of 320 feet (a Jumbo Jet's is 197 feet). It was supposed to carry loads of soldiers and supplies from the USA to Europe, to win World War II. But Spruce Goose flew only once, for 2950 feet in 1947. It's been stored in a hangar at Long Beach, California ever since.

The Mackerel car

In the 1960s a Swedish inventor came up with a car that had numerous sausage-shaped balloons around each wheel. An air pump and valves controlled their inflation and deflation. On each wheel they blew up the sausage just behind the one flat on the ground, and let down the sausage in front.

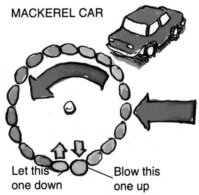

MACKEREL CAR

Let this one down

Blow this one up

Do this fast, and hey presto, the wheel rolls forwards! No one took up the idea.

The mini-skirt

Skirt hemlines have gone up and down through the ages. In the early 1960s, fashion designer Mary Quant unveiled the miniskirt. It was very short and used less material, yet it often cost more than a long skirt! Some people said it was fun, others said it was daring or disgraceful. Miniskirts have come in and out of fashion since.

The Zike – will it, won't it?

The Zike was launched in spring, 1992. This two-wheeled bike has an electric motor and rechargeable battery, and a top speed of 12 mph. Anyone over 14 can ride it on the road without a special licence.

Some people say that the Zike will alter our lives. Maybe. Guessing about the next invention that will change the world is all part of the fun.

INDEX